Bob Marley

BY IAN McCANN

ISBN: 0.7119.3550.5 Order No: OP47384

Exclusive Distributors
Book Sales Limited, 8/9 Frith Street, London W1V 5TZ, UK.
Music Sales Corporation, 257 Park Avenue South, New York, NY 10010, USA.
Music Sales Pty Limited, Lisgar House, 32 Carrington Street, Sydney, Australia, NSW 2000, Australia.

To the Music Trade only:
Music Sales Limited, 8/9, Frith Street, London W1V 5TZ, UK.

Photo credits: All photographs courtesy of Adrian Boot

Printed in the United Kingdom by Ebenezer Baylis & Son Limited, Worcester.

A catalogue record for this book is available from the British Library.

OMNIBUS PRESS
LONDON · NEW YORK · SYDNEY

CONTENTS

INTRODUCTION

When Omnibus asked me to write this book, apart from being flattered, I was filled with a decidedly un-natty dread. Getting a handle on Bob Marley's catalogue is a mammoth task, never mind attempting to say something about it. However, someone has to do it, and it might as well be me. Marley is the major international artist in reggae, and one of maybe half a dozen 'rock' acts to whom you can always return and find the music as fresh as ever. On some occasions, one or other of his albums may sound terrible. In a different mood, you'll understand it. There's always at least one Marley album that can move your soul: you've just got to select the right one. Hopefully, this book will help you choose.

Apart from listing the albums, I've tried to clear up some of the mysteries that have bewildered Marley fans and collectors for years. Undoubtedly, in doing so, some of the information contained in this book will contradict the information to be found in others. There are some stories that were written once in one newspaper that have been reprinted repeatedly in others, when the original stories probably were not true. Where possible, I have tried to clarify these stories as best I can. The 'Soul Revolution II' album is a case-in-point: just why did the vocal album come out in what appears to be the sleeve of the dub LP? It's a small mystery to collectors, which redoubles when you consider that the dub album probably didn't actually have a sleeve in the first place... other queries, such as where the tracks from Trojan's 'In The Beginning' LP *really* come from, whatever the sleevenote might say, are also, hopefully, definitively answered. And just what was the Tuff Set label anyway? Collectors will, I hope, be fascinated. If you're not a Marley obsessive, but own one of the many compilations and are looking for guidance towards more of the same, this book is for you too.

Dates. As anyone who looks into reggae history at even the slightest depth can testify, it's a far more complicated business than the rock world. Labels come and go, artists record for hundreds of them over a long career, and, even when you're face to face with someone who was there at the time, that doesn't mean that they're going to remember what came out when. Maybe they'd recorded for three different companies that month. Maybe they'd recorded the same *song* for three different companies that month. Months turn into years, and, without the constant nudging of an A&R department or a press office that constantly reminds a rock artist just where he is in his career, firm information about a reggae act gets forgotten. In the end, all we, and they, can do is guess.

One thing I would say, however, is that some discographies place records at altogether too early a date. Hence we're sometimes led to believe that rocksteady records were recorded in 1965 (impossible) or that Bob's ska was two years ahead of anyone else's. It is also often said that UK single releases of Bob's '60s material can be up to two years behind the Jamaican releases. They may be six months behind in some cases, but otherwise the idea is laughable: the people in the UK reggae record business were, by and large, fully conversant with the scene in Jamaica, and many of them (such as Rita & Benny King, who ran the Ska Beat label) also owned popular record shops. Records were being imported into the UK from Jamaica then much as they are today. Can we really expect the owners of a shop to not release a popular record in the UK for years, long after the demand for it has dried up on import? Of course not.

Dates, where I've been able to mention them, are merely guesses, but they are informed guesses, comparing the sound of the records with other records released at the time. They are, of course, double-checked as much as possible with higher authorities, such as those present at the time, other books and magazines, and a bunch of experts in England. They may not all be right, but they are as right as I can get them.

Marley's songs speak for themselves with a rare eloquence. Their origins do not. Hence, in the case of 'Keep On Moving', or 'Stand Alone', for example, the reader is directed towards earlier influences, earlier songs, or, regrettably, earlier writers. I hope it doesn't cause too many lawsuits! Estimates of authorship are only estimates in some cases. It was not uncommon – it still is not uncommon, unfortunately – for reggae producers, who also owned the studios, record labels and publishing companies for whom an artist might work in Jamaica, to keep their artists in the dark about the mysteries of publishing. Hence, you'd find an album such as 'African Herbsman' largely licensed from Lee Perry for release in the UK, and the writers' credits nearly all go to the producer. Perry may have written all the songs he is credited with on the sleeve,

I don't know. But if so, then why does the 'Kaya' album, which contains three of the same songs, credit them to Bob Marley? Ownership of writer's credits is a minefield in reggae.

Beyond all this, there is the music. Marley's is a catalogue far bigger than many realise, and I guarantee you that on every album that comes out in his name you'll find something (maybe not everything, but in some cases, everything) that will lift your spirits. Marley may or may not have been the saint some have portrayed him to be. Marley may have been a shrewd businessman, a sharp dealer. Marley may have been the most honest man in music. He may have been a womaniser, or he may just have had a lot of love to give. He may have been a prophet, or just another minstrel with a knack for a deep-sounding song. It doesn't really matter any more. What does matter is the music. That music speaks for itself. I hope that this book helps you to hear what it is saying.

Ian McCann, October 1993

ACKNOWLEDGEMENTS

A heartfelt thanks and love to Joan, my wife, and Sam & Kitt.

This book would not have happened without the invaluable assistance of Noel Hawks, an unacknowledged authority, perhaps *the* unacknowledged authority, on reggae music. Without his help and patience, this confusing, frustrating, annoying volume would not have arrived in the shops. Blame him. I am!

I am indebted to the following persons for their expertise, whether they know it or not: Chris Charlesworth & his patience; Paul Coote, a man-to-man solver of obscure mysteries; Danny Kelly, someone who doesn't know how to say no even in wet weather; Trevor Wyatt and his cardboard box; Rob Partridge's remarkable memory, Gaylene Martin; Nick White and the Famous Canadians; S. Mudgegrove; my editors at *NME, VOX, Music Week, Billboard, Zit* and elsewhere; John MacGillivray, Pat, Hortense, and everyone at Dub Vendor; Chris Lane; Judy Mowatt; Family Man; Everyone at Tuff Gong; The Bob Marley Foundation; Carl Bradshaw; Gillie Dread; Harry Hawke; Chris Blackwell; Rod Hull & His Emu; Prince Paul;

Bunny Lee; Lee Perry; The Third Ice Cream Man; Baby Fish; David Corio; Father Tim Finigan; Dot at Trojan; Dixie & Susan, Steve Lamacq, Andrew Collins, Patrick Humphries. All those of you whose brains and expertise I have picked endlessly over the years: you know who you are.

Thanks and love to my Mum & Dad.

The following books have been mercilessly plundered and misunderstood. The writs are in the post: *Catch A Fire* by Timothy White (Omnibus); *Bob Marley* by Stephen Davis (Doubleday); *Bob Marley, Soul Rebel, Natural Mystic* by Adrian Boot & Vivien Goldman (Eel Pie/Hutchinson); *Bob Marley In His Own Words*, by Jove (Omnibus); *Heavy Streggae A Leggo* by Professor Winifred Morgan (Labrish).

BOB MARLEY – THE MAN

Bob Marley was born Robert Nesta Marley in Nine Mile, St Anns, Jamaica, on February 6, 1945, the son of an English army captain and a God-fearing Jamaican country girl. He was moved to a poor area of Kingston, Jamaica's capital, by his mother while still a young child. In the early Sixties the youthful Marley was, like every other ghetto kid, excited by the nascent Jamaican music industry, and in 1962 made his first record, 'Judge Not', for producer Leslie Kong's Beverly's label. It was not a hit, and neither were two follow-ups, 'One Cup Of Coffee' and 'Terror'.

Marley then formed a vocal group, starting with his friend Neville O'Riley Livingston, better known as Bunny Wailer (b. 1947), and then adding a feisty youth, Peter Tosh (Winston McIntosh, b.1944), and Junior Braithwaite, a younger singer with a voice like an untutored Motown-era Michael Jackson. Beverly Kelso was also part of the fold. Cherry Green, Constantine Walker, Marlene Gifford, and later, Rita Anderson were also to appear on record at various points in these early years.

Calling themselves The Wailers, they fashoned themselves after American vocal groups, such as The Impressions and The Drifters, although their first records, recorded under the auspices of producer Clement 'Sir Coxsone' Dodd at his Studio One building in Brentford Road, Kingston, and mostly issued on Dodd's Studio One label, were pure Jamaica, with none of the smoothness of American soul. 'Simmer Down' was the first hit (1964), followed by 'I Am Going Home', 'Mr Talkative' and many more. By 1965 Junior Braithwaite had quit in order to start a new life in America, and Beverly Kelso was soon to quit too. Now basically a three-piece, The Wailers continued to score local hits, and their harmonies were now tight enough to compare with any of their Jamaican contemporaries, even if they didn't get the studio time that the American acts were granted. Marley, Tosh and Livingston swapped lead chores, and all had plenty to offer, with Marley doing his best to sound like a sock-it-to-'em soulman, Tosh providing a raw, disdainful bark, and Bunny offering a tender, mellow tone guaranteed to melt the heart of their female following. Hits like 'Rude Boy', 'Lonesome Feeling' and the remarkable R&B lilter, 'I'm Still Waiting', reinforced their grip on Jamaican youth, although, in truth, they were

just one of many acts scoring huge hits in the ska era. Their first album, 'The Wailing Wailers', was issued around this time.

Marley married Rita Anderson, who had just begun a recording career herself with The Soulettes, in February 1966, and went to live in Delaware in order to earn a decent living. Bunny and Peter continued to record as The Wailers, cutting many sides, including 'Who Feels It Knows It', 'Let Him Go' and 'Rolling Stone', gradually adapting from the fury of ska to the milder tempo of rocksteady. Marley returned in October of that year, and the trio almost immediately began work on their own label, Wail'N'Soul'M.

Although they recorded a slew of majestic rocksteady sides for the label between 1967 and 1968, including 'Nice Time', and the original versions of 'Bend Down Low' and 'Don't Rock The Boat', the label met with little success. Marley began to write for Johnny Nash, an American singer who had discovered the charms of reggae before most of his compatriots, and Marley, sometimes with The Wailers, recorded sporadically under the production supervision of Nash, his manager Danny Sims, and producer Arthur Jenkins and their JAD

label. Bunny reputedly served a short jail sentence around this time for possession of dope.

In 1969 the trio turned to Marley's first producer, Leslie Kong, and cut an album's worth of songs for his Beverly's label. The records were not a success, and the group was reportedly displeased when Kong issued them on album as 'The Best Of The Wailers'. They cast around for other producers, recording for Dynamic and Bunny Lee in 1969-70, before settling with reggae maverick Lee Perry for the space of two albums, 'Soul Rebels' and 'Soul Revolution' (1970/1). Perry brought out the best in the group, offering a sparing, funky backdrop for what were, by now, rebellious, outlaw lyrics and searing harmonies. They cut several of their best songs with him: 'Small Axe' and 'Duppy Conqueror' among them. They also filched his rhythm section, the Barrett brothers, Aston and Carlton, as formidable a bass and drums team as has existed in black music the world over.

At the same time Marley continued his alliance with JAD, resulting in a trip to Europe in 1972 and abortive recording sessions in London. Marley also had his own label in Jamaica, Tuff Gong, on which wonderful Wailers records would appear with increasing regularity, such as 'Trenchtown Rock' (1971) and 'Lively Up Yourself', (1972). In 1972 The Wailers ran into Chris Blackwell, owner of Island Records, who had released Marley's first single and a heap of the group's Studio One material in England. Blackwell signed the group, and they released two albums, 'Catch A Fire' and 'Burnin'', which in 1973 were both marketed like the rest of Island's rock catalogue. The group toured England and America for the first time, although the jaunt was also to prove their last: Bunny disliked road life and quit in 1973. Likewise Tosh was also dissatisfied, and he too quit the band. Both would concentrate on their own labels (Solomonic and Intel Diplo HIM) and release some strong records for years to come. International success was on its way for Bob, however, when Eric Clapton had an American No 1 with a world-weary cover of 'I Shot The Sheriff', a song that débuted on 'Burnin''.

Marley enlisted the help of Rita for vocal support. She, in turn, drew in Marcia Griffiths and Judy Mowatt, both solo singers in their own right, to form The I-Threes, who would do backups from now on. In 1974 Bob Marley & The Wailers released 'Natty Dread', a fresh, self-possessed album full of striking songs and arrange-

ments, and saw the first glimmers of chart action in Britain. 1975's 'Live!' and attendant single, 'No Woman, No Cry' was the real breakthrough, and from this point on virtually all Marley's albums, and many of his singles, were hits.

However, it wasn't to be plain sailing. In December 1976 Bob was shot at in his Kingston home by raiders unknown. While in exile, he cut two of his best albums, 'Exodus' (1977), and 'Kaya' (1978). A toe injury sustained during a football match turned cancerous, and in 1977 a skin-graft operation provided (temporary) respite.

A sporadic, but collectively impressive string of hits continued, among them 'Waiting In Vain', 'Jamming' (1977), 'Is This Love' (1978) and 'Could You Be Loved' (1980). However, Marley found America a hard nut to crack, and in particular black radio stations did not always get behind him, often considering him to be a rock act – if they thought about him at all. In April 1978, he brought warring factions together in Kingston at the legendary Peace Concert, getting Prime Minister Michael Manley and Opposition leader Edward Seaga to embrace onstage in an attempt to stop political bloodshed in Jamaica. In 1980 he played the Zimbabwe Independence celebrations. Marley was a world figure, but was probably unable to do all he wanted in, and for, a poor Jamaica as a result of international demands.

While on tour of America in 1980, a drawn-looking Marley collapsed whilst jogging in Central Park, New York, and a brain tumour was diagnosed. He moved to Bavaria to undergo treatment at the clinic of Dr Josef Issels, but eventually flew to Miami to die, on May 21, 1981.

A controversial, sometimes roughneck, often tender figure, Marley was not an easy man to sum up. His commitment to Rastafarianism was well-known, as was his liking for beautiful women. The two are not necessarily incompatible, as his music, offering both philosophical and physical love, makes clear. He left behind many children from different mothers to carry on his work, among them Ziggy Marley & The Melody Makers, and a thriving Tuff Gong, now a distribution company and pressing plant as well as a record label. The Bob Marley Foundation, a charitable organisation, maintains his vision for a better deal for Jamaica's ghetto youth. And for the rest of the world, Bob Marley has left his music, a unique, unequalled catalogue of uplifting songs, still moving hearts the world over ∎

STUDIO ONE RECORDINGS

'THE WAILING WAILERS'

(STUDIO ONE S1001, JAMAICAN OR AMERICAN VINYL IMPORT ONLY, 1965)

Rarely, if ever, out of press since its first release, this legendary compilation of The Wailers' Sixties singles material for Studio One, Jamaica's Motown equivalent, remains extremely alluring today, despite the availability of much of the material elsewhere on what are almost inevitably better-mastered CD versions.

As the sleeve declares, here are "Jamaica's Top-rated Singing Sensations accompanied by THE SOUL BROTHERS", i.e. whoever was playing in the session band for producer Clement 'Coxsone' Dodd on the days that Bob, Bunny & Peter, plus a variety of other vocalists, were recording. (Not all the tracks were recorded with The Soul Brothers who were, technically speaking, led by keyboard player Jackie Mittoo, but other bands, such as The Skatalites, The Mighty Vikings and The Sharks were involved.)

A wild, crazy mix it is too, tracing The Wailers development from a wild, style-free group with something to say, through wobbly but still emotive doo-wop and pop covers, to a silky R&B-styled vocal group almost the match of The Impressions, probably The Wailers' main influence. Wrapped in one of two equally-legendary sleeves, one a lot rarer than the other, occasionally in monochrome and more often in full colour, 'The Wailing Wailers' remains an authentic document of its time, a feeling that the slapdash nature of the whole album only enhances rather than detracts from it. Those seeking pristine sound and packaging can purchase Heartbeat's 'One Love' compilation or Epic's 'Birth Of A Legend' set. If you want it the Jamaican way, warty pressing'n'all, here it is.

Producer: Clement Seymour Dodd, AKA 'Coxsone' Scorcher Dodd. Musicians: from Jackie Mittoo, Lloyd Delpratt, Danny McFarlane, Richard Ace (kbds); Marley, Tosh, Jah Jerry, Ernest Ranglin, Lyn Taitt, Dwight Pinkney, Hux Brown, Ranny 'Bop' Williams (guitars); Lloyd Knibbs, Esmond Jarrett, Carl McCloud, Lloyd Robinson (drums); Lloyd Brevitt, Lloyd Mason, Lloyd Spence, Fred Crossley, Bryan Atkinson (bass); Roland Alphonso, Tommy McCook, Tony Wilson (tenor sax); Headley Bennett, Lester Sterling, Seymour Walker (alto sax); Carlton Samuels, 'Ska' Campbell (baritone sax); Jonny 'Dizzy' Moore, Bobby Ellis, 'Trummie' Miles, Leonard Dillon (trumpet); Don Drummond, Vin Gordon, Ron Wilson (trombone); Roy Richards, (harmonica). Singers: Bob Marley, Bunny Wailer, Peter Tosh, Junior Braithwaite, Beverly Kelso, Constantine 'Vision' Walker, Cherry Green, Rita Marley Anderson, Marlene 'Precious' Gifford.

NB, for all Studio One albums and compilations: Jamaican single pressings mentioned are usually Studio One or Coxsone. Although these labels are the ones normally associated with reissues and hence the easiest to find, in fact the producer (who, in true reggae fashion, also owned the studio and record and publishing companies) would press Wailers' material on a variety of labels including the above, and World Disc, Supreme, Wincox, and Music City.

PUT IT ON
MARLEY

A spiritual from 1965 with Bob leading Bunny and Peter through one of the most tender and assured harmony performances of their early career. Although its content is apparently strictly religious, 'Put It On''s attitude is not, conversely, at odds with their more physical 'rude boy' material of the same era. The "I rule my destiny" line is not so very different from the stance of 'Rude Boy's "Walk the proud land with me". Both infer a sense of self-determination of the sort common in a ska music that grew almost directly from Jamaica's wilful struggle for independence. Also probably the first record to introduce the concept of toasting, as in "I'm not boasting, I just... feel like toasting." Also released on the British Island label as a single (WI 268, 1966).

I NEED YOU
MARLEY

A simple doo-wop song from 1965 with sore, regretful lyrics and harmonies to match. Bob leads the group, and the backing-voices of what sounds like a four-piece Wailers, including Beverly Kelso, show an early sharpness of the sort sometimes to have only arrived at the turn of the Seventies. Also released on the 'One Love' compilation. There is another 'I Need You' in The Wailers' Studio One catalogue, a tearaway ska tune.

'Lonesome Feeling' (Marley).

The first genuine ska track on the album, driven along by Jackie Mittoo's pumping organ and punctuated by a bright, punchy trumpet solo. Although this is early Wailers (1964-5) and the harmonies are as awry as anything they did, the sheer enthusiasm of the group connects every time, as does the logic of the writing: these people really knew how to write even at such an early stage. Line-up reputedly includes Bob, Bunny, Peter, Junior Braithwaite, Beverly Kelso and second female vocalist Cherry Green. Also released on Ska Beat 7 in the UK (JB 211), credited as The Wailers with The Mighty Vikings.

WHAT'S NEW PUSSYCAT
BACHARACH/DAVID

A cover of the Tom Jones hit from the film of the

same name. No-one in The Wailers bothers much about sounding like the fabulous Welsh belter, however, nor are they concerned with getting the chord changes right, preferring instead a honking ska horn section, Jackie Mittoo's R&B piano licks and an altogether gentler lead vocal from Bob. Also a UK single on the Island label (WI 254 1965).

ONE LOVE
MARLEY

Although 'Put It On' was the first Wailers' classic on the album to be cut again and again, 'One Love' has an even more enduring appeal, providing Bob with a posthumous UK hit in 1984 and offering a demand for unity that remains strongly appealing today – enough for Heartbeat to name their Wailers compilation after the track, as well as providing obvious resonances in other musical spheres, such as presumably inspiring British groove-pop band One Dove and giving The Stone Roses a song title. Bob's internationalist, multi-cultural persona comes through loud and clear here: this is a career in the making in itself. Bunny shares the lead vocal. Issued on UK Island (WI 268), remixed with disco bassdrums and added percussion by Coxsone Dodd in the wake of Bob's 'Exodus' version for an Eighties Studio One 45, the original remains, nevertheless, the definitive cut. Not to be confused, incidentally, with Peter Tosh's 'Rasta Put It On', a different song altogether.

WHEN THE WELL RUNS DRY
TOSH/LIVINGSTON

Back to the tender doo-wop, with a rolling, steady R&B rhythm, 'When The Well Runs Dry' follows the proverbial line taken from American gospel and soul (Sam Cooke, Otis Redding), comparing a love affair with liquid nourishment. Mild, never hectoring, Bunny and Peter's lead vocals and the faintly simpering harmonies from Rita and Constantine 'Dream' Walker add up to a surprisingly effective track.

TEN COMMANDMENTS OF LOVE
M PAUL

The Moonglows' harmony classic rendered faithfully in a dirt-slow version led by Bob. Fantastic ethereal vocals at the end are sometimes obscured by clicks and pops, depending on your luck with the pressing.

RUDE BOY
THE WAILERS

"Walk the proud land" with the rudies, dance the "ska quadrille" and demand some soul. A plain, good-time ska classic, it holds overtones of youth revolution and helped kick off reggae's rude boy legends, a perennial topic in the music. Lead vocal from Bob. Also released on Studio One and UK Doctor Bird (DB 1013, 1966) Lee Perry also used the same rhythm track for his 'Pussy Galore' single (Studio One) in which The Wailers sang support, a sign that Coxsone's recording equipment was running to a two-track tape recorder by now.

IT HURTS TO BE ALONE
MARLEY

Junior Braithwaite leads The Wailers through a record not only unique in the Marley canon, but also in the whole of reggae. A ballad, 'It Hurts To Be Alone' runs on a logical, circular set of jazzy chords while The Soul Brothers lay down a gentle beat. Come the middle eight, guitarist Ernest Ranglin lets go of a clear-toned solo that explains precisely why he was held in such high esteem in Jamaica at the time: it would stand up with America's finest. Still an under-appreciated classic, released on UK Island as a single (WI 188, 1965) and available in an alternate take on Heartbeat's 'One Love' album.

LOVE AND AFFECTION
MARLEY

Marley was once quoted as saying that 'Love And Affection' (sometimes called 'Love Or Affection') was perhaps the first serious song that he wrote, although it's possible he may have been speaking in a commercial sense, since, with the craftiness of a Brill Building employee, he manages to work the titles of several previous Wailers hits into the lyric – 'Lonesome Feeling' and 'It Hurts To Be Alone' amongst them. Reputedly a favourite on The Wailers' occasional Sixties live outings, it's a solid, warm song rather than an absolute stunner. Also on UK Skabeat (JB 228, 1966).

I'M STILL WAITING
MARLEY

However, 'I'm Still Waiting' *is* an absolute stunner, and no mistake. The Wailers in soul mode, with Bob bemoaning the fate of unrequited lovers worldwide. Far better than the other songs of the title, this record oozes pure class, even if it does,

sadly, seem to finish without reaching the end. There's a reason for this, and you can hear the full version in an alternate take on Heartbeat's 'One Love' set – even Jamaican pressings of the single lack the final minute or so for no apparent reason. Covered in the early Seventies by Delroy Wilson, and in the mid-Seventies by Cornell Campbell, it's still the original, however, that brings wistful tears to the eyes of those who knew it in their Jamaican youth, and rightly so. Also a single on Studio One/Coxsone (JA), and this version appears on the 'Songs Of Freedom' set.

SIMMER DOWN
MARLEY

The first Wailers hit in Jamaica, reputedly cut in 1963 although by the sound of it, late 1964 seems a more likely date. British single release (Ska Beat JB 186) didn't occur until 1965. Taken at a belting pace that only youth – both of the group, and of ska itself – could cope with, 'Simmer Down' is a plea for even-temperedness in a Jamaica already coming under the hypnotic glint of the rude boy's ratchet. A real ska stormer that must have come like a shot from a gun out of Coxsone's Downbeat sound system whenever he played it at the time.

'BEST OF BOB MARLEY AND THE WAILERS'
(COXSONE/STUDIO 1 FCD 1-7, 1974)

Although the title is certainly an exaggeration, 'The Best Of Bob Marley & The Wailers', another Jamaica/US import-only, available sporadically in various sleeves, certainly has more than its fair share of stunning performances. Drawn from The Wailers' work at Studio One, with one exception, 'Small Axe', this has a strong claim to be the match of 'The Wailing Wailers', although it lacks a little of its predecessor's coherence and concentrates more on rocksteady material than ska.

Although the title is certainly an exaggeration, 'The Best Of Bob Marley & The Wailers', another Jamaica/US import-only, available sporadically in various sleeves, certainly has more than its fair share of stunning performances. Drawn from The Wailers' work at Studio One, with one exception, 'Small Axe', this has a strong claim to be the match of 'The Wailing Wailers', although it lacks a little of its predecessor's coherence and concentrates more on rocksteady material than ska.

'The Best Of...', like all of The Wailers' Studio One albums, suffers from poor pressing and erratic mastering, but if you want the authentic Jamaican feel, here it is. Sleeve was printed in various colours (but only one per copy!) with the silhouette of Bob, Bunny & Peter stolen from 'Burnin''s cover. Perhaps due to an intervention from Island Records, it was later given another sleeve, drawn by New York artist Jamaal Pete, who also created the sleeve for 'Marley, Tosh, Livingston And Associates'.

Producer, musician and artist credits as per 'The Wailing Wailers'.

I AM GOING HOME
MARLEY

Cut in 1964/5, and fronted by Bob, while behind him a five-piece Wailers, including Beverly Kelso and the unappreciated Junior Braithwaite, get happy. 'I Am Going Home' is another from the 'Simmer Down' pot of wild ska and cut at the same session. Unlike 'Simmer Down', however,

'I Am Going Home' is concerned more with biblical events than a rude boy's temper, and just about hints at the philosophy that would come to fruition on 'Exodus'. Blasting away on a considerable horn section and what is presumably Lloyd Knibbs' clattering snare drum, it's hardly subtle, but it hits the spot all the same.

BEND DOWN LOW
MARLEY

By way of a total contrast comes the song that Bob recut for the 'Natty Dread' album. Although recorded at Studio One, this piece of vaguely risqué rocksteady ("Bend down low, let me tell you what I know") was in fact amongst The Wailers' first recordings for their own Wail'N Soul'M company, issued in Jamaica on that label (1967), and in Britain on Island (WI 3043) as singles. The production has all the stately hallmarks of The Wailers' short-lived, self-produced rocksteady. Far better than the more well-known version.

MR TALKATIVE
MARLEY

Bob attacks a gossip, offering physical violence – to the point of murder! – to shut a loose-lipped mouth. A rough ska tune, punctuated by what sounds like Roland Alphonso's fluid tenor solo, and one of the few Marley songs to sound like it was actually written by a rude boy rather than just observing the actions of one. This version was cut in 1965, issued on UK Island as a 7" (WI 188) and Bob also recorded it in a more playful style for producer Bunny Lee in 1969 available on the 'All The Hits'/'Nice Time' LP.

RUDDIE

Also known as 'Jailhouse', under which title it came out in Britain on the Bamboo label (BAM 55, 1970), and as 'Good Good Rudie' (Doctor Bird DB 1021), this was one of the last truly great Wailers records for Studio One (1966). A paean to the rising youth of Jamaica, a plea for restraint and wisdom in the face of provocation, a biblical declaration of prophecy and even a very graphic mention of physical love all in one. Bob's "Baton sticks get shorter, ruddie gets taller", line is a small masterpiece in itself. The final line, oft-repeated in reggae, "What has been hid from the wise and prudent is now revealed to babes and sucklings", is lifted wholesale from the Bible (Matthew 2:25, Luke 10:21).

Somehow, the seemingly diverse subjects all

work perfectly well together, as Bob apparently outlines all the things important to him at once. A real sign of spiritual growth when compared to the early material, and if that isn't enough, there's also a delicate, understated trombone solo at the end and some tear-jerking harmonies at the fade-out that you wish had gone on forever.

Lead singer: Bunny. This track also appears on the 'One Love' LP. Also recorded by Bunny Wailer for his 'Sings The Wailers' album, and if you can get it, there's a Studio One instrumental single version (harmonica!) of Roy Richards' 'Green Collie', that's a fine complement to this cut.

CRY TO ME
MARLEY

Similar to 'Ruddie', 'Cry To Me' (1966) takes a similar formula, only this time we're in pure doo-wop loneliness-emptiness territory. Not so much a song as a ramble, even including a little of the 23rd Psalm (a perennial reggae favourite) although Peter and Bunny's harmonies really are tear-jerkers. There's some evidence, in Bob's "What's that?" and his occasional soul shouts, that this is the start of The Wailers' mild obsession with becoming James Brown-style reggae

soulsters, a Wailers backwater that reached high-tide-point on the 'Soul Rebels' album. It doesn't entirely work here, but Bob returned to the song on the 'Rastaman Vibration' album, where his vast experience made more sense of an undisciplined tune. There is, incidentally, on some pressings at least, a unique opportunity to hear Bob clearing his throat of a tickle after the rest of the song is finished. Since the music fades out before the rest of the group, we can safely assume that 'Cry To Me', as is 'Ruddie', was one of the first Wailers songs to be recorded without the band being there at the same time. Whether this means they were using a random backing track that Dodd happened to have available is unclear, but it may explain the rambling nature of the song. Also released on the 'One Love' LP.

WINGS OF A DOVE
TRADITIONAL

The folk spiritual given a tender ska work-out, with the voices right up front as they are on much of The Wailers' later Studio One stuff. Charming, even if it is once again a little undisciplined, as if, by the time this was recorded at Mr Dodd's little Brentford Road studio (1966), The

Wailers were so confident of their prowess that they were cutting stuff like this, first or second take. No shortage of magic here though, since Bob's lead vocal is spot-on, and the lazy crooning harmonies have plenty of character.

SMALL AXE

This was written by Marley, or Perry, or Marley/Perry depending on what you believe. Not actually 'Small Axe' as such, although the *song* is certainly 'Small Axe'. How this wound up on a Studio One album is anyone's guess, since it is, as the sleeve admits, "Courtesy Upsetter Records". Hence, this track is about five years younger than its album-mates, and it shows. A purposeful, crisp skank, this is in fact a second version of 'Small Axe', originally released as 'More Axe' following the original's Jamaican success in 1971. The difference? 'Small Axe' has horns and is taken at a more urgent tempo, while this version is far more laid-back. If you can't find this version, you'll also find the song on 'The Very Best Of The Early Years 1968-74'. The other version is also on the same album, and 'African Herbsman'. 'More Axe' was issued on UK Upsetter 7" (US 369, 372), with an instrumental version on the flip, 'The Axe Man', in 1971.

LOVE WON'T BE MINE

The full, five or six-piece Wailers, fronted by Bob circa 1965, aims at the sort of post-doo-wop of Garnet Mimms & The Enchanters, replete with Beverly Kelso's high end harmonies and Peter Tosh's bass voice. The song is a dismissal of an old girlfriend and one of the slighter items in The Wailers' catalogue. Issued on UK Island 7" (WI 268).

DANCING SHOES
MARLEY

Bunny leads Bob and Peter through a simple, logically structured ode to good times, which suddenly raises itself to a higher level for the middle eight. The Wailers' harmonies were never better than this, lifting the honking ska backbeat far beyond what it deserves. A classic, still well-remembered in Jamaica, and recut by Bunny for his 'Sings The Wailers' album. Also issued on the British Rio label as a 7", (R116, 1966).

SUNDAY MORNING
LIVINGSTON

Another Bunny tour-de-force, 'Sunday Morning' is one of the gentlest, slowest, most accomplished love songs ever recorded in Jamaica, capturing the glorious romance of a hot Sabbath in Jamaica like nothing before or since. Also recorded by Gregory Isaacs for Bunny's own DANSCI label in 1980, but the original remains the definitive version, (UK Island 7" WI 3001, 1966).

HE WHO KNOWS IT FEELS IT
MARLEY

"Every man thinks his burden is the heaviest," suggests Bob on a topic subsequently returned to in reggae many times. Another gentle ska-going-rocksteady song from a group easily able to out-gun the competition with sheer confidence if the layered vocals are any indication at all. They make it look easy. Also on UK Island (WI 3001) as the A-side to 'Sunday Morning'.

STRAIGHT AND NARROW WAY

Back to the early ska era (circa 1964) with The Wailers, fronted by a very junior-sounding Junior Braithwaite, again offering moral advice to the rudies and wayward female acquaintances. Not wonderful, but it has a finality that closes the album adequately.

THE WAILERS: 'MARLEY, TOSH, LIVINGSTON & ASSOCIATES'
(STUDIO 1 FCD 4041, 1982)

The third and final compilation to date of material put together by The Wailers' first producer lacks the obvious logic of the first two and comes across as a bit of a mish-mash. Released in 1982 with a passable if unsophisticated Jamaal Pete painting of an older, dreadlocked Wailers on the cover, it's hard to work out why Dodd selected these particular tracks for reissue: Dodd certainly has no shortage of other available material, although perhaps these songs were just the closest to hand when he was putting the album together. These reservations aside, there are some stunning moments, even if the mastering is decidedly short of bite. And any album with a sleevenote that begins: "Hello there" and ends with "It gives great contribution to this being a very outstanding album" must have something going for it.

One point in its favour is the explanation as to who is singing what, something that the previous Studio One albums could have done with. Unfortunately, something that this album could have done without is a remix, which it got. Supervised by the original producer, and subtle compared to 'Chances Are' and the vinyl pressing of 'Birth Of A Legend', this is, nonetheless, tampering with perfection. If you can stand the added percussion and vaguely discoish bass-drums somewhere in the bottom of the mix, it's worth buying.

ANOTHER DANCE
MAYFIELD

Bob returns to the joys of meeting someone at a dance, courtesy an Impressions song. A light, easy ska workout from 1965/6.

LONESOME TRACK
MARLEY

Considering that Jamaica's railway service is limited to say the least, the number of reggae songs about trains is excessive, perhaps because of the influence of R&B and soul train-songs, and the locomotive pull of Curtis Mayfield's 'People Get Ready', which unites soul harmonies with gospel sentiment. Marley, no stranger to either, demands of the Lord "Why must man suffer?" as the gospelling Wailers answer with "Get on board". These are the same sentiments that would later come together in their cover of the gospel tune 'This Train' ('One Love', 'In The Beginning' LPs). 1966, also issued on UK Ska Beat (JB 249).

ROLLING STONE
LIVINGSTON/DODD

Marley meets Dylan, sort of. Although few have said as much, there seems little doubt that Dylan's Seventies conversion to Christianity and songwriting with apocalyptic vision circa 'Slow Train Coming' was influenced by Marley's rise to fame. Likewise The Wailers must have felt the American Bob's pull at a distance in the Sixties. Bunny leads the group through an adaptation of some of Dylan's greatest hit, with a particularly Jamaican edge to some of the new lyrics: "Time like scorpion stings without warning". Unusual acoustic Latinesque guitar, perhaps from Ernest Ranglin, again suggests a folky influence. The interesting thing is, this was recorded in 1964, a year before Dylan's version. On holiday in Jamaica in January 1965 he saw The Wailers live at the Carib Theater... only kidding. 1966. Bunny later redid it as 'Ballroom Floor' for his 'Rock 'n' Groove' album (1981). Interestingly, The Wailers 'Sinner Man', from 1967, was erroneously titled 'Zimmerman' on some single pressings.

CAN'T YOU SEE
TOSH

Rock and roll? From The Wailers? Superficially, Tosh's 'Can't You See' appears to be a Sixties rocker, but chances are this is simply because the clanging guitar appears too high in the mix, giving a faintly distorted edge. It is far more likely they were aiming for a Motown feel in 1966, particularly in the shape of Lloyd Knibbs' machine-gun snare fills and hustling (years before the hustle) hi-hats. Perhaps feeling that the song didn't get justice, they tried again for producer Leslie Kong in 1969 ('The Best Of The Wailers'), and Peter had a crack at it on his 'Mystic Man' album (1979). It's a shame that Mr Dodd, with the rights to release some Motown material in Jamaica (his own "The sound of young Jamaica" logo was a direct rip off of Motown's "The Sound Of Young America") couldn't somehow engineer a visit to Detroit for his young band. Chance would be a fine thing. This song also appears on the 'One Love' set, in a much more audible form.

LET HIM GO
LIVINGSTON

AKA 'Let Him Go (Rude Boy Get Bail)'. Bunny pleads for the bonded release of a framed rude boy over a ska-turning-rocksteady track, warning the authorities to "Remember he is smart, remember he is strong, remember he is young and he will live long". With the pungent aroma of its time (1966) in every carefully-delivered line, this somehow seems like more than just another Wailers hymn to the underdog: it's almost a prophecy of a revolution to come – a social revolution to find a focus in Rastafarianism for The Wailers. This is Bunny and Peter, incidentally, while Bob was living in Delaware. Also issued on UK Island (WI 3009).

DANCE WITH ME
MARLEY

Although credited to Marley and given fresh lyrics evocative of long, steamy nights in Kingston, this 1965 recording is an adaptation of two hits – 'On Broadway' and 'Dance With Me' – by another Wailers' influence, The Drifters. The band is as tight as a ska producer's wallet, the voices waste nothing, and the overall effect is of something mildly marvellous fashioned from very little.

MAGA DOG
TOSH

Tosh fronts one of his signature tunes for the first time, a curt, totally unsympathetic dismissal of an old girlfriend on a rough ska rhythm. "When I was with you, you was big and fat, now you look like a railway track". From 1966 and issued on Island UK (WI 212), Tosh later did it over in 1971 as a single for Joe Gibbs with amended lyrics, in 1972 for his own Intel Diplo label, and on his 1983 'Mama Africa' album. His son, Andrew, also took up the theme on 'Same Dog Bite You All Morning' in 1987.

I WANT SOMEWHERE
MARLEY/DODD

Bob searches for a place to call his own – a roof over his head, Heaven, or a return to Africa? – on a few gospel songs melded into one ska whole from 1966. The opening couple of lines – "I've been rebuked, brothers, and I've been scorned" – have appeared repeatedly in black music since before the music business realised that there was such a thing.

HOOT NANNY HOOT
ADAPTED TOSH

Tosh fronts a dance song drawn from traditional folk sources, as he did with 'Jumbie Jamboree' (a 1965 single based on 'Zombie Jamboree'). The responding harmonies are raw but engaging, the music is rough hewn 1965 ska, and the do-ce-do adapts as well here to The Wailers' style as does the quadrille in 'Rude Boy'. Released in the UK on Island (WI 211), credited to Peter Touch & The Wailers. Since many Jamaicans pronounced *Tosh* as *Touch*, that's how the credit came about. The name stuck for several releases.

DREAMLAND
LIVINGSTON

Like 'Small Axe' in 'Best Of Bob Marley & The Wailers', 'Dreamland' stands out like a sore thumb from Marley, Tosh, Livingston And Associates, although this time the song, virtually Bunny Wailer's anthem, *was* cut at Studio One (1966). Bunny is not only promising the romance of living in a world of love to a woman here, he's also evoking, for one of the first times of many in reggae, a better time for black people in a dreamland known as Africa. The natural life offered by the coda – honey from the bees, breakfast from the trees, eternal life – remains one of the strongest sentiments in reggae.

The Wailers returned to the song definitively for Lee Perry in 1971, and Bunny remade it for 'Blackheart Man' (1976, also issued on Island and Solomonic 45s), 'Dub D'sco' (1978) and 'Sings The Wailers' (1980) albums. There's also two DJ versions of the Lee Perry cut, U Roy's 'Dreamland' (UK white label 7" only circa 1972), and 'Vision Land' by Istan (Solomonic, 1975). Marcia Griffiths, one of The I-Threes, also recorded it for her 'Naturally' LP. Exactly where this cut first saw light of day, however, is a mystery to the author.

BOB MARLEY & THE WAILERS: 'ONE LOVE'
(HEARTBEAT HB111/112, TWO CD SET, 1991)

One Love is simply a wonderful compilation celebrating the Studio One material of one of the finest vocal groups of all time.

With 40 tracks, mastered almost entirely from original masters, 'One Love' sets such a pace it's hard to conceive of a similar compilation coming along to top it. With three unreleased tracks and a bunch of alternate takes, this comprehensive trawl through the archives is a must for anyone seeking the roots of the sound that Marley took to the world.

THIS TRAIN
TRADITIONAL

An unreleased take of The Wailers' favourite spiritual supported only by acoustic guitar. Bunny & Peter only, recorded 1966. Later done on The Wailers own Wail'N Soul'M' label as a 45, a further version, produced at Dynamic, is to be found on the 'In The Beginning' LP.

SIMMER DOWN Details: 'The Wailing Wailers' LP **I AM GOING HOME** Details: 'The Best Of Bob Marley &The Wailers' LP. This version is slightly longer than previously issued editions.

DO YOU REMEMBER

AKA 'How Many Times', this is a subtly-rhythmed ska side with Bob on lead vocals, previously issued on UK Island (WI 211, 1965) and on the Melodisc 'Honeys' compilation, and in Jamaica on the 'This Is Jamaica Ska' LP (Studio One).

MR TALKATIVE Details: 'Best of Bob Marley & The Wailers'. Also on 'All The Hits' LP as 'Mr Chatterbox'.

HABITS

Featuring a chorus of Bob, Bunny, Peter, with Cherry & Beverly Kelso and a very young-sounding Junior Braithwaite on lead vocals, 'Habits' is the sort of folk-song of advice that innumerable ska artists tried their hands at.

AMEN
TRADITIONAL

The spiritual, fronted by Tosh in ska style. Also covered by Wailers' idols The Impressions, which is perhaps why they wanted to do it.

GO JIMMY GO

A ska dance tune borrowed from a Jimmy Clanton song of the same tune. Bob sings lead. The track also turns up on a Studio One/Melodisc various-artists album, 'Jamaica Ska'/'Honeys'.

TEENAGER IN LOVE
MARLEY

Almost Dion's famous 'Teenager In Love', but not quite. The verses, tackled by Bob and Peter, differ considerably from the Doc Pomus/Mort Shuman song. The backing is a two-beat R&B rhythm with a choppy guitar from either Peter or, possibly, Ernest Ranglin. Also a UK single on Ska Beat (JB 228), 1966.

I NEED YOU Details: 'The Wailing Wailers'. One of a couple of songs of the title that The Wailers cut. In error, the sleevenote for this album appears to believe that this version is the hard ska one, rather than the aching doo-wopper.

IT HURTS TO BE ALONE Details: 'The Wailing Wailers'. This is a different take, with a different, but equally gorgeous jazz guitar part from Ernest Ranglin.

TRUE CONFESSION

Previously unreleased. Another ska jump-up, a shade more subtle than the preceding titles. Bob kicks the song off, but a five-piece Wailers, including Beverly Kelso and Junior Braithwaite, take part.

LONESOME FEELING Details: 'The Wailing Wailers'. This master features a brief false start.

THERE SHE GOES
MARLEY

Another two-beat R&B/doo-wop tune, fronted by Bob with some pretty unharmonious harmonies from the entire six-piece group. Fantastic cinema organ, however, from someone whom history has forgotten – probably not Jackie Mittoo, since this was credited on single to The Wailers & The Mighty Vikings. Also a single on UK Ska Beat (JB 211, 1965). The song, although different, probably forms a basis for 'Stand Alone' ('Soul Revolution'/'African Herbsman' LPs) since its subject matter and lyrics contain several similarities.

DIAMOND BABY
MARLEY

Rough, rough, rough. Over a fierce Skatalites backing track of the sort that wouldn't disgrace a Don Drummond solo session, The Wailers fire off a punchy adaptation of Curtis Mayfield's 'Talking 'Bout My Baby'. Released on Jamaican single, but only just, judging by the number of copies that have turned up.

PLAYBOY

Unreleased alternate take of the ska song that turned up on single on UK Island (WI 206, 1965). Part of it, in typical Wailers style, is another composition: The Contours' Motown smash 'Do You Love Me'.

WHERE'S THE GIRL FOR ME

The other side of 'Diamond Baby' on single, a slow, regretful doo-wop with another fine guitar solo from Ernest Ranglin.

HOOLIGAN

A crack at rioting rudies. "Hooligans hooligans make up your mind," bark Bob, Peter and Bunny, evoking a scene of broken bottles and weeping mums. UK Island single (WI 212, 1965).

ONE LOVE Details: 'The Wailing Wailers'
LOVE AND AFFECTION Details: 'The Wailing Wailers'.

AND I LOVE HER
LENNON/McCARTNEY

Giants meet giants: an adaptation of The Beatles' ballad. More enthusiastic than masterly, but an interesting curio. This unreleased take is an alternative to the one to be found on the original Jamaican single release.

RUDE BOY Details: 'The Wailing Wailers'. Curiously, although this is not supposed to be a different version, on this master the rimshots seem more powerful than on the album cut, and the piano less punchy than on the original single. It also fades out a little early if it is the previously-released version **I'M STILL WAITING** Details: 'The Wailing Wailers'. Another unannounced alternate take, with Marley's vocal far more upfront and the whole far longer than previously anthologised.

SKA JERK
MARLEY

A furious ska belter, with The Soul Brothers band

in fantastic, smouldering form on the repeated riff and King Sporty, later to turn up in Bob's posthumous story for 'Buffalo Soldier' (see 'Confrontation' album) giving true 'Chain Gang' style "Oooh-ahhs" in the background. Bob does the jerk as well as any of his soul contemporaries, on the evidence of this. Bob's other jerk tunes include 'The Jerk' and 'Jerk In Time'.

SOMEWHERE TO LAY MY HEAD AKA 'I Want Somewhere'. Details: 'Marley, Tosh, Livingston and Associates'.

WAGES OF LOVE REHEARSAL

Previously unreleased. A couple of minutes of what sounds like Peter and Bob on acoustic guitar and vocals, learning a song with female singers of questionable identity.

WAGES OF LOVE

The 7" Jamaican single release of previous entry. A poppy R&B tune with brushed snare and rather soggy guitar.

I AM GONNA PUT IT AKA 'Put It On'. Alternate take with more guitar and reverb on the drums. Details: 'The Wailing Wailers' **CRY TO ME** (Bob's biblical love ballad) Details: 'The Best Of Bob Marley & The Wailers' **JAILHOUSE** AKA 'Rudie' and 'Good Good Rudie'. Details: 'The Best Of Bob Marley & The Wailers'.

SINNER MAN
TRADITIONAL, LATER CREDITED TO TOSH

AKA 'Zimmerman'. The original rocksteady/ska version of the incendiary gospel warning Peter would return to repeatedly as 'Down Presser'. Impressively glum and righteous, Peter and Bunny both sing lead. This take is faintly different from the one on single. Also a single on UK Island (WI 3009, 1966), and Ska Beat (as 'Zimmerman', JB 249, 1966). They cut it again with Lee Perry as 'Down Presser' (Peter Touch, The Wailers, UK Punch PH77, JA Upsetter, 1971, the latter with a dub version on the flip). Tosh did it as 'Downpressor Man' on his 'Equal Rights' album (1977), and 'Captured Live' (1984).

WHO KNOWS IT FEELS IT Details: 'The Best Of Bob Marley & The Wailers' **LET HIM GO** Details: 'Marley, Tosh, Livingston & Associates'. **WHEN THE WELL RUNS DRY** Details: 'The Wailing Wailers'. **CAN'T YOU**

SEE Details: 'Marley, Tosh, Livingston & Associates'. This master is far crisper.

WHAT AM I SUPPOSED TO DO
LIVINGSTON

Bunny fronts a gloriously elegant rocksteady-ska love song with a delicious sax solo from Tommy McCook. Almost the match of, and very similar to, Delroy Wilson's massive hit 'Dancing Mood', cut at the same time (1966) for Studio One.

ROLLING STONE Details: Marley, Tosh, Livingston and Associates'. This master is far clearer and has not been remixed. **BEND DOWN LOW** Details: 'The Best Of Bob Marley And The Wailers'.

FREEDOM TIME
MARLEY

AKA 'Children Get Ready', this haughty-rhythmed rocksteady tune was originally cut for the 'Wail'N Soul'M' label as the flip of 'Bend Down Low'. A fantastic performance from Bob, rising in strength as the song goes on. A little-known Wailers' classic, some of which was rehashed for 'Crazy Baldhead' ('Rastaman Vibration' album). Also released on UK Island (WI 3043, 1967).

ROCKING STEADY
MARLEY

The basic version rather than the overdub-cluttered pressing usually found on Coxsone Jamaican 45, released in the mid-Eighties. A simple four-chord ode to the joys of rocksteady dance with Bob singing lead, Bunny, Rita and Peter in support. No-one seems to know for certain when it was recorded: the sleevenote suggests 1971, although Coxsone's studio sound was usually far more sophisticated than this by that time. Its true origins are a mystery, and the track is perhaps not actually a Coxsone production at all: it sounds more like a Johnny Nash/JAD demo. That's only a theory – not mine, I hasten to add, but that of an informed source – but one that sounds extremely plausible. If that's the case, this would date from around 1968, the rocksteady era – hence the subject-matter. After all, if it was cut in 1971, why would Bob be extolling the virtues of a dance that died three years ago? The song, incidentally, is an adaptation of 'Calypso Cha Cha Cha' by Count Lasha & His Calypsonians (Jamaican Caribou 78 RPM single, circa 1958).

BOB MARLEY & THE WAILERS: 'THE BIRTH OF A LEGEND', AKA 'BIRTH OF A LEGEND 1963-66'
(CALLA CAS 1240, 1976; EPIC ZGT 46769)

A compilation of Studio One oldies, first issued – and sadly tinkered with, sound-wise, by famous disco producer Tom Moulton– in 1976 on the Calla label. The CD remastering in 1990 for Epic put the sound problem straight. Extensive, informative sleevenote by Timothy White, author of Catch A Fire: The Life Of Bob Marley, on the CD release. In 1977 CBS also issued the Calla LP in two halves, as 'The Birth Of A Legend' and 'Early Music', credited to Bob Marley & The Wailers, featuring Peter Tosh. Tracks were also drawn from the LP for a budget-price LP on the Hallmark label, 'Bob Marley & The Wailers with Peter Tosh'.

I MADE A MISTAKE
MAYFIELD

A cover of an Impressions song that finds The Wailers in regretful doo-wop mode. Released on Ska Beat 7" in the UK (JB 226 1965). A low-key opener.

ONE LOVE Details: 'The Wailing Wailers' **LET HIM GO** Details: 'Marley, Tosh, Livingston & Associates' **LOVE AND AFFECTION** Details: 'The Wailing Wailers' **SIMMER DOWN** Details: 'The Wailing Wailers' **MAGA DOG** Details: 'Marley, Tosh, Livingston & Associates' **I AM GOING HOME** Details: 'The Best Of Bob Marley And The Wailers'

DONNA
MARLEY

A rough, untutored ska tune, cut in 1964.

NOBODY KNOWS
TRADITIONAL

Nobody knows the trouble Bob has seen on yet another ska side. Of average quality, although the trumpet solo halfway through is strong enough.

LONESOME FEELING Details: 'The Wailing Wailers' **WINGS OF A DOVE** Details: 'The Best Of Bob Marley And The Wailers' **IT HURTS TO BE ALONE** Details: 'The Wailing

Wailers' **I'M STILL WAITING** Details: 'The Wailing Wailers' **WHO FEELS IT** AKA 'Who Feels It Knows It'. Details: 'The Best Of Bob Marley And The Wailers' **DO YOU REMEMBER** Details: 'One Love' **DANCING SHOES** Details: 'The Best Of Bob Marley And The Wailers'

I DON'T NEED YOUR LOVE
MARLEY
A rough, raucous ska'n'B tune with untutored, over-enthusiastic harmonies.

LONESOME TRACK Details: 'Marley, Tosh, Livingston & Associates'

DO YOU FEEL THE SAME WAY
Bob wonders if she cares on a reasonable but unexciting ska tune.

THE TEN COMMANDMENTS OF LOVE
Details: 'The Wailing Wailers'.

'CHANCES ARE'

(WEA K99183 UK; COTILLION SD 5228 US. 1981)

Following Bob's death in 1981, there was an unseemly scramble among labels totally unassociated with him in his lifetime to put out something with his name on it. 'Chances Are' was the album that drew the most attention, perhaps because it was at least on a major label with a good deal of media muscle. And it also contained material which most of Bob's public would not have been aware of, unlike literally dozens of other compilations which merely juggled the 'Soul Rebels'/'Soul Revolution'/'Best Of The Wailers' material ad nauseam.

Recorded between 1968 and 1972, the eight tracks on 'Chances Are' were cut for JAD, the label owned by Danny Sims, Johnny Nash's manager. Marley became involved with Nash and Sims in 1968, and supplied a heap of songs for Nash that gave Bob his first taste of international success. Marley also signed to Cayman Music, Sims' publishing company, but rumours have it that Bob was so discontented with his Cayman deal in the Island era to credit his songs to Rita, bandmembers, or friends from Trenchtown rather than see them published by Cayman. Whatever the truth of this, there is no denying that Sims was the first businessman with international connections smart enough to see that Bob could make it beyond Jamaica.

That said, 'Chances Are' is not a great album by any stretch of the imagination. Doctored in the studio years after they were recorded, the majority of the tracks have had guitars, drums, backing vocals, horns and percussion added. Hence, simple songs like 'Soul Rebel' and 'Dance Do The Reggae' become big-production numbers. As for 'Reggae On Broadway', it's one of Bob's first attempts to win himself an American audience, but it's easy to see why it failed. Doubtless Sims deserves credit for spotting Bob's potential and making it clear that there was a whole world out there waiting to be conquered. However, if 'Chances Are' was the standard by which Bob's potential was to be judged, then he would never have made it. Given modern studio technology, it's possible to make a silk purse from a sow's ear, as 'Iron Lion Zion' proved. Maybe Sims should have another crack at it.

Producers: Bob Marley & Larry Fallon. Executive producer: Danny Sims. Original producers: Danny Sims, Johnny Nash, Arthur Jenkins.

REGGAE ON BROADWAY

Unfortunate, really, that the LP should start with 'Reggae On Broadway', because this rock-funk mixture is a terrible abortion, leaving Bob's voice hanging thinly in everything from fuzzbox chords to a sitar run. The original version, on CBS single (8114, Britain only), was far less fussy, if undistinguished. This cut was issued as a 12" single on Cotillion.

GONNA GET YOU

This is more like it, in that any added stuff, apart from the Rasta drumming, is pretty unobtrusive and what we can presume to be The Wailers' harmonies are in full effect. It won't go down as classic Bob, but it's pleasant enough. Also issued as the flip to the rehashed 'Reggae On Broadway'.

CHANCES ARE

The title track is a slow, southern-styled soul ballad, with Bob and (probably) Rita doing their William Bell & Judy Clay bit.

SOUL REBEL

The original version of the title track to a later LP. At least, it would be the original, had it not been turned into a big-production number with Sly Dunbar-style drumming and phased guitar.

DANCE DO THE REGGAE

Bob as early-Seventies uptown soulman, with disco overdubs and even some reggae thrown in.

MELLOW MOOD

One of Bob's first writing successes for Johnny Nash gets a cluttered remake. The original is to be found on 'Songs Of Freedom'. The JAD version (ie this one minus overdubs) was a single coupled with 'Bend Down Low' as Bob Marley Plus Two (WIRL, JA, JAD US), and turns up on several compilations, among them 'Soul Rebel' on New Cross Records (UK) and 'Jamaican Storm' (Accord, US).

STAY WITH ME

What was probably a rocksteady tune at first is given some Rasta drumming and two-beat militant reggae snare. The production for the original, such as it is, sounds curiously like the work of Leslie Kong. Otherwise, Bob's voice sounds flat in places, suggesting this was a forgettable demo.

I'M HURTING INSIDE Details: 'Songs Of Freedom'. This version is laden with overdubs.

'SOUL REBEL'
(NEW CROSS NC 001/BELLAPHON)

Sims/Nash/Jenkins-produced tracks without overdubs, issued in the UK on New Cross, and Bellaphon in Germany in 1982. Far better than 'Chances Are', but a very low-key release. This material has been re-pressed on various labels under different titles throughout the world so often that it has become almost valueless to Marleyphiles.

Tracks are: 'There She Goes', 'Put It On', 'How Many Times', 'Mellow Mood', 'Changes [Chances] Are', 'Hammer', 'Tell Me', 'Touch Me', 'Treat You Right', 'Soul Rebel'.

'JAMAICAN STORM'
(ACCORD US SN7211)

The same album as 'Soul Rebel' on New Cross/Bellaphon.

These are by no means the only pressings of this material. Other albums of the same material include 'Treat You Right', 'Mellow Mood', 'Hammer', 'Trenchtown Rock' etc.

'BOB, BUNNY, PETER & RITA - BOB MARLEY AND THE WAILERS'
(JAD JR 10002, 1985)

More JAD productions from the late Sixties with additional instruments.

Tracks: 'Oh Lord' AKA 'Oh Lord I Got To Get There', 'It Hurts To Be Alone', 'Lonesome Feelings', 'Milkshake & Potato Chips', 'Touch Me', 'Lonely Girl', 'The World Is Changing', 'Treat You Right', 'Soul Shake Down Party'.

LESLIE KONG (BEVERLY'S) PRODUCTIONS

THE WAILERS: 'THE BEST OF THE WAILERS'
(BEVERLY'S BLP 001, CIRCA 1970)

In 1969 The Wailers did some recording sessions for Leslie Kong. Kong, at the time, was reggae's most internationally successful producer with Desmond Dekker, Jimmy Cliff and Toots & The Maytals, amongst others. Bob had recorded three or four songs for Kong in 1962-3 before The Wailers formed, to little acclaim. (See the 'Songs Of Freedom' box set.) Likewise The Wailers' late-Sixties material, largely recorded at Dynamic Sounds studio in Kingston for Kong's Beverly's label, didn't click with the reggae-buying public, and this later association was short-lived, with the feisty trio of Bob, Bunny & Peter soon finding a more sympathetic foil in producer Lee Perry.

The Leslie Kong sessions are a melding of rock-steady and the emergent reggae beat, with considerable influence from funky southern soul in the improvised interjections, and have been repackaged umpteen times by innumerable licensees in Europe and America until their familiarity has made them appear eminently contemptible. If you can't find them under this title, try 'Shakedown', 'Soul Shakedown Party', 'Best Sellers', 'Soul Captives', etc. The material will inevitably be the same.

Since no-one has bothered to protect the exclusivity of the material, you might assume that it's hardly the best of The Wailers, and you'd be right. Few of these songs were revisited by the group for their major-label careers. However, there are some wonderful moments here, which Marley fans miss at their peril.

SOUL SHAKEDOWN PARTY
MARLEY

The best-known song from these sessions, Bob's 'Soul Shakedown Party' is a demand for fun with strong harmonies and a chugging rhythm typical of the era. Bob does his best to offer some of American soul's atmosphere, adding "Huh" like Edwin Starr or Wilson Pickett here and there, and crying "Hit it brother y'all" before what sounds like Winston Wright's organ solo. The (perhaps apocryphal) story goes, incidentally, that The Wailers and Kong cut this tune together in a co-operative deal but that Kong reneged on the agreement. The song also appears on the 'Songs Of Freedom' set, and on two Trojan UK 45s, (TR 7759, 1970; 7911, 1974). The former boasts an instrumental version on the flip credited to Beverly's All Stars.

STOP THE TRAIN
TOSH

Tosh fronts another train song, sounding genuinely hurt at emotional and social injustice. Perhaps influenced by Keith & Tex's huge rocksteady hit of a similar title, 'Stop That Train'. Tosh liked the song enough to tackle it again for the 'Catch A Fire' album (1973) and his 'Mama

Africa' album (1983). This original version was a Summit UK single (SUM 8526 1971).

CAUTION
MARLEY

The best record The Wailers made for Kong, 'Caution' rolls on a descending staccato guitar lick from Hux Brown, of the sort that often enlivened a Leslie Kong production. Another request for restraint, comparing life – and The Wailers ongoing search for the ultimate in black music – to a road in varying states of repair and weather conditions: "Caution the road is wet, black soul is black as jet, caution the road is hot, said you gotta do better than that..."

It was reportedly written after Bob spent a night in jail after being pulled up in his car while Rastafarian leader Mortimer Planno was driving without a licence. The harmonies are nothing short of delicious, and even Bob's "Hit me from the top, you crazy muthafunkin'" doesn't sound out-of-place. That line is deleted from the UK Summit 45 (SUM 8526, 1971) in a rare example of reggae censorship. Here's The Wailers as soul rebels, performing as some have erroneously believed they could only work after tuition from Lee Perry, their next producer. The song also appears on the 'Songs Of Freedom' set and came out as the flip to 'Soul Shakedown Party' on UK Trojan (TR 7911).

SOUL CAPTIVES
MARLEY

Another Wailers record verging on gospel, fronted by Bob, with more tremulous guitar licks from Hux Brown and a slavery sentiment that shows their growing Rasta consciousness. Once again, the backing vocals are beyond compare.

GO TELL IT ON THE MOUNTAIN
TRADITIONAL

Tosh fronts a version of the spiritual, apparently adapted by Marley if the writing credits are to be believed, which they probably aren't. It has its moments, particularly in Tosh's smouldering, occasionally flaming lead.

CAN'T YOU SEE
TOSH

Tosh and The Wailers return to the rocking song of their Studio One era, with not much discernible improvement, since here, despite the snare fills of Winston Grennon and Winston

Wright's organ, everything seems to drag. The original is on 'Marley, Tosh, Livingston & Associates' and was later remade by Tosh for 'Mama Africa' (1983).

SOON COME
TOSH

Tosh again, bemoaning the non-arrival of what may be a girlfriend but is probably an unreliable, non-paying business acquaintance. The title is a Jamaican saying demanding both patience and supplying a brush-off, much taken up by rock journalists writing about reggae in the Seventies. Despite warm, jazzy guitar chords, this is a bit of a space-filler. It was a Jamaican single on the Beverly's label, backed by an instrumental cut (1970). Tosh did it again for his first Rolling Stones Records album, 'Bush Doctor' (1978).

CHEER UP

A predecessor of 'No Woman No Cry', and a son of Sam Cooke's 'A Change Is Gonna Come', without the magic of either, despite the inevitable ethereal harmonies. The line "We've been down in captivity so long," was later adapted by Bunny Wailer for his excellent 1981 single, 'Rise And Shine'.

BACK OUT
MARLEY

Perhaps the second best Kong-Wailers collaboration after 'Caution', 'Back Out' has the folksy air of the 'Catch A Fire' sessions. Bob's not pretending to be an American soul singer here, instead singing the praises of some round-the-way girl and putting down someone who dares to interfere, in a purely Jamaican fashion. A casual classic with a fine organ solo that deserved a revisit circa the Kaya album but never got one. The song also appears on the 'Songs Of Freedom' set.

DO IT TWICE
MARLEY

Bob loves her, but she won't let him. She's "So nice, he'd like to do the same thing twice." Whatever can he mean? As easy as 'Back Out', even if it isn't its match, just tossed off as casually as a dry beer can, giving the impression that The Wailers weren't trying as hard for Kong as they knew they could. Also on the 'Songs Of Freedom' set.

LEE PERRY PRODUCTIONS

In 1970 or thereabouts The Wailers arrived under the production wings of Lee Perry. Perry, a notorious reggae maverick, had worked with The Wailers before at Studio One, where both learned their trade. In fact, The Wailers had sung harmonies on his rude 'Pussy Galore' single (1966), and Rita's group, The Soulettes, had also supported Perry's own creaky, but faintly Bob-like voice. All split from Studio One boss Dodd at around the same time in 1967, and Perry had found considerable success as one of the new breed of independent producers, along with Bunny Lee, Derrick Harriott, Joe Gibbs and several others, in the late Sixties.

Since Perry was interested in fusing funky American music with reggae, exploring the feelings of a Jamaica becoming increasingly aware of its attitudes towards Rastafarianism and black militancy – themes which fascinated The Wailers – it became inevitable that the two parties would team up. Working out of Randy's Studio 17 on North Parade, Kingston, and occasionally Dynamic Sounds, The Wailers and Perry cut in excess of two-albums' worth of songs, largely released on Perry's own Upsetter label. The liaison also gave Bob the basis of a band in the shape of The Upsetters' rhythm section, brothers Carlton 'Carlie' (drums) and Aston 'Family Man' (bass) Barrett. Other musicians on the sessions included Glen Adams (keyboards), Hux Brown (guitar) and Lloyd 'Tinleg' Adams.

BOB MARLEY & THE WAILERS: 'SOUL REBELS'
UPSETTER TBL 126 1970; TROJAN TBL 126 1970, REISSUED 1989

Although in some ways similar to The Wailers' material for Leslie Kong, there were crucial differences in that Perry's production offered a minimalist, no-frills approach which brought out the best in Bob's writing: the songs stood or fell on their own merits. Here are the basics of the whole sparing skank movement of the early Seventies, the emptiness of dub, and in parts, the music that Bob would bring to the world through Island Records, although here he seems to be freewheeling naturally rather than sitting down writing a song. The sleeve features a semi-nude black woman in front of a Jamaican waterfall, probably shot against a backdrop in a grimy London attic, clutching a very heavy-looking machine gun. Sex and revolution: two major aspects of Marley's oeuvre in one shot! The reverse has The Wailers standing on a rock, baby dreads hidden under hats, their shirts faintly hippie-looking African prints.

Produced by Lee Perry. All songs written by Bob Marley according to the credits. Likely differing authorship in brackets.

SOUL REBEL

The Wailers as strangers, gossiped about, the sort of people that parents warn their kids about: "I'm a capturer... that's what they say." But Bob declares himself to be a "Living man", in touch with the natural world. It's the natty dread as outsider stance, later to find a slight adjustment in 'Natty Dread' itself. Behind him the band offer what must, then, have seemed like ridiculously little support, and although the harmonies are as strong as ever, they seem almost irrelevant compared to Bob's upfront message. The rhythm track was later used to construct The Wailers 'Run For Cover', the flip to the first Tuff Gong 45 ('Sun Is Shining'), Glen Adams' 'Rebels Version' (Capo), Jacob Miller's 'I'm A Natty' (Reflections JA) and I Roy's 'Knotty Knots' (Town & Country JA) singles in 1975. Bob also cut the song, circa 1969, for JAD Records ('Chances Are' LP).

TRY ME

Bob as loving protector soul man over a faintly funky backing track with a rolling, ascendant bass line typical of Aston Barrett's work at the time. The drums are almost inaudible, as they are on a lot of the tracks on the album, but it doesn't seem to matter, since everything on the track is purely rhythm anyway. Not the James Brown song, incidentally.

IT'S ALRIGHT

Another funky tune, this time certainly the sort of thing that James Brown might have constructed – right down to the "If it's all night, got to be alright" middle-eight – had Brown been a ganja-fuelled Jamaican natty dread. Bob returned to the song as 'Night Shift' on the 'Rastaman Vibration' album (1976).

NO SYMPATHY
TOSH

Tosh on a deep, rootsy rhythm track with cluck-ing guitar, outlining his troubles and lack of sympathetic love. A singularly gloomy, mesmeric track, also issued on a white label 45 in England. Tosh also offered a reasonable remake on his début solo LP, 'Legalize It' (1976).

MY CUP

Marley has lost the best friend he ever had, he complains from within the recesses of an over-used reverb unit over a typically busy but some-how empty Upsetters rhythm track. The cup he's referring to is a cup of tears, and this sounds sus-piciously like a demo despite Marley's go-for-it attack on notes that seem faintly beyond his reach. Also issued as a single on the British Upsetter label (1970, US340), and the rhythm track was put out as 'Version Of Cup' (US342).

SOUL ALMIGHTY

The Wailers, chiefly Bob, do the funky chicken and mashed potato on a slight song about their ownership of rhythm. This owes such a huge debt to American soul that it's a wonder that Rufus Thomas didn't slap out an injunction on it for appropriating his style – or at least, attempt-ing to.

REBELS HOP
MARLEY/WHITFIELD-STRONG

During 1970 and 1971 a brief craze swept through reggae for medleys, and many acts attempted one. The Wailers did two, this being the first, 'All In One' (on the 'African Herbsman'

LP) being the other. This one matches 'Rude Boy' (from 'The Wailing Wailers' LP) with a version of The Temptations' 'Cloud Nine', which The Wailers may or may not have had a crack at with Lee Perry (on 'Best Of The Upsetters Volume 2' LP, with uncredited singers, Jet Star UK). A bit of a pointless exercise, but Bunny's singing on 'Cloud Nine' is wonderfully gentle.

CORNER STONE

Jamaica is sometimes colloquially known as 'The stone that the builder refuse', a Biblical reference (Psalm 118), and Marley extends the metaphor to relationships, saying that he may have been turned down but he can be the corner stone of someone's happiness. A warm, pleasant track, reliant on the tender harmonies to come across.

400 YEARS
TOSH

Tosh turns his attentions to mental slavery: 400 years on, it's about time black people rose up. Not, as is often assumed, an attack on white oppressors, but instead a rallying cry for the oppressed. Tosh sounds suitably furious. To turn up a couple of years later, recut, on the 'Catch A Fire' LP.

NO WATER

Supported by soaring and purring trills from Bunny and Peter, Bob has a thirst that can only be quenched by a nurse. A wet nurse, judging by the lyric. A small gem, in that Bob gets straight to the point and the arrangement is wonderful.

REACTION

Another slight, freestyling song, lyrically related to 'Don't Rock My Boat' (AKA 'Satisfy My Soul'), which Marley cut the following year. Once again Bob's talking about soul, with a slur in his voice – and the groove – that suggests a good few spliffs during the session.

MY SYMPATHY

Although the title leads the listener to believe that this is a version of 'No Sympathy', it is, in fact, an instrumental of '400 Years'.

BOB MARLEY & THE WAILERS: 'SOUL REVOLUTION', AKA 'SOUL REVOLUTION II'

JAMAICAN UPSETTER TTL65A/TTL65B; JAMAICAN MAROON LOPTTL65B/TI65A, ALSO ISSUED ON US BLACK HEART. DATE AS BELOW.

After sailing casually through their first album with Lee Perry, the second set is an altogether more organised affair with a few songs that later became very famous indeed. The obsession with matters soulful takes a back seat, replaced by a rougher, more determinedly Jamaican stance. Released in 1971... perhaps (see next entry).

Produced by Lee Perry. Writer: chiefly Bob Marley, although the sleeve of 'African Herbsman' with many of the same tracks, credits Lee Perry for almost all of them. Guesses at correct authorship, other than Marley's, in brackets.

KEEP ON MOVING
MAYFIELD

Not, as many assume, a Marley composition, and certainly not written by Perry as 'African Herbsman' suggests, but actually written by Curtis Mayfield and first recorded by The Impressions (on their 'The Never Ending Impressions' album, 1965). However, by the time Bob, Bunny and Peter have taken a verse each (Bunny's closing stanza is particularly marvellous) The Impressions might as well concede defeat. A vocal tour-de-force, and probably the reason why Bob wrote 'I Shot The Sheriff': the storyline is remarkably similar. 'Keep On Moving' also influenced 'Rude Boy' ('The Wailing Wailers'). There's an alternate take to this version on 'The Upsetter Record Shop Part II'. Perry later put Big Youth on the backing track for 'Moving (version)' (UK Upsetter US 393, JA Justice League 7" singles, 1972). The producer took the original vocal version, added a honking sax and a DJ called Wong Chu, and dubbed the track into oblivion for a 12" single on the Jamaican Upsetters label in 1977. Bob covered it again with new lyrics in 1977, available on 'Songs Of Freedom', which also turned up on a 1984 EP fronted by 'One Love'. Finally, Bunny cut it for his 'Sings The Wailers' LP (1980).

DON'T ROCK MY BOAT

The song that Marley later had a hit with as 'Satisfy My Soul' from the 'Kaya' LP (1978), here in its original, minimal skank form, unsupported by harmonies of any kind. A quietly perfect, self-contained track. Also known, on slightly different single releases, as 'Rock My Boat' (JA Tuff Gong single, 1971, with a different vocal), and with a DJ version by Johnny Lover on the flip, ('I Like It Like This', UK Supreme single, 1971, another vocal again). The first version was 'Don't Rock The Boat' on Wail'N'Soul'M 45, circa 1968.

PUT IT ON

Another version of the song they'd already done in 1966 (on 'The Wailing Wailers' LP). This version reduces the music to a hypnotised background and pumps the vocals, almost all harmonies except for the very occasional Marley interjection, right up front. The song later showed up on 'Burnin' (1973).

FUSSING AND FIGHTING

A demand for harmony in the sweetest tones. Glen Adams' organ pumps away and up front Bob gets considerably animated. A song that

deserved another version, which it never got.

DUPPY CONQUEROR V/4

'V/4' because this is the fourth version of the song, a true Marley classic, although you wouldn't really know it from the mostly instrumental mix here. See 'African Herbsman'.

MEMPHIS
TOSH

Around the time of working with Lee Perry, Peter Tosh was also cutting various instrumentals on either organ or melodica for a variety of producers ('Selassie Serenade', 'The Return Of Al Capone', 'Sun Valley'). Hence, although 'Memphis', a melodica instrumental, perhaps seems out-of-place on a largely vocal album, it's consistent with Tosh's then-current career moves. Augustus Pablo later made this sort of thing into an artform. Here, it's a mildly pleasant diversion.

RIDING HIGH
LIVINGSTON

Bunny fronts 'Riding High' in what was a regrettably rare lead outing at the time. He's chasing a girl and is patient enough to wait for her to come around to him in what is a deliciously simple, homely ode to a reluctant love. Bunny later did it again as 'Riding' as a single (Solomonic, 1981) and on 'Hook, Line & Sinker' (Solomonic LP1982).

KAYA

The ode to herb that later formed the title track on a 1978 Marley LP here gets a far more subtle, laid-back stoned-sounding first outing. The whispering here and there indicates the fact that they're doing something illegal, the ethereal harmonies make it clear just what it is they're doing. Also released as a British single as 'Kayah' (US356, 1971), and also on a Jamaican Upsetter 45. The American pressing of the single on Upsetter features different harmonies. Bob did another song on the backing track as 'Turn Me Loose' in 1974 ('In The Beginning', 'Very Best Of The Early Years' LPs).

AFRICAN HERBMAN
HAVENS

Correct title: 'African Herbsman'. Richie Havens' song gets a slightly different angle through Jamaican eyes: "Herbman" implies marijuana, and therefore, in concert with the other half of the title, suggests Rasta. The song could almost have been written for Bob, with its references to slavery and the bit about grinding your corn slowly, reminiscent of the "everything in its own time" philosophy often found in Bob's writing. Not recognised as a Wailers classic, but it should be. Also issued on UK (US392, 1972) and Jamaican Upsetter singles and forms the title of a Trojan LP.

STAND ALONE

Another tender, gentle love song, this time dealing with regretful memories, from Bob, with fine support from Bunny & Peter. The lines "Here you are crying again, but your loveliness won't cover your shame," sum up the to-the-bone personal nature of the subject matter. It also formed the flip to 'African Herbman' (sic) on an obscure US-pressed single on the Black Heart (sic: correct title, Black Art) label (1974). Ziggy Marley has covered it as 'There She Goes' on 'Joy And Blues' (Ghetto Youths United, Jamaica 1993). That's a clue as to where 'Stand Alone' came from in the first place: lyrically, and thematically, it's akin to 'There She Goes', a Wailers 1965 ska song (on 'One Love' LP). Marley wastes very little as his career continues.

SUN IS SHINING

A strange record, perhaps closer to the stuff on 'Soul Rebels' than its surroundings here. Since the lyrics make no lucid sense, we can assume that there's a certain amount of improvisation going on here. As for the title, also the first line, no melody could be less sunny than this. However, Bob cut it again for the 'Kaya' LP, and it was a UK 45 in its original form as 'To The Rescue' (Escort, 1970). DJ Johnny Lover also released a cut on Tuff Gong 7" as 'Sun Is Shining', circa 1971. Rumour has it that his version was also credited to Jah Talla, but I've yet to see hard evidence.

BRAIN WASHING
LIVINGSTON?

Bunny gets to grips with the rubbish you're told as a kid, discarding nursery rhymes and fairy stories. Although this probably has resonances in every culture, to a Rasta who believed in mental slavery, it had all the more impact. His seems to have been the only version of the song, except on the following album.

BOB MARLEY & THE WAILERS: 'SOUL REVOLUTION II'
JAMAICAN UPSETTER TTL65/66A/B, UK TROJAN 2 WHITE LABELS TTL65A/B; 66A/B

Confusion reigns amongst Marley historians regarding this album. Some clarification is required.

The legend: producer Lee Perry, looking to capitalise on the Jamaican success of 'Soul Revolution', pressed up a 'dub version' of the album, called 'Soul Revolution II' in 1971. This is not actually dub as we now know it, but really just the instrumental tracks, which could pass for dub in poor light, since they were pretty minimal and bass-heavy anyway. Perry had plenty of sleeves made, and when the limited pressing of the dub album ran out (perhaps just 250 were made), continued to sell the vocal album in the dub sleeve, which was a different colour (blue) to the original (turquoise), and also featured colour photographs whereas the original had black and white.

However, that story may not actually be true. An equally-plausible version runs thus: Perry makes the 'Soul Rebels' LP of Wailers tracks. Trojan put it out in England in 1970, then ships the stampers out to Perry, who presses it up with a facsimile of the UK sleeve and the same matrix number as Trojan's, on his Upsetter label (certainly true). The record does not sell particularly well. Perry, frustrated that a record he considers to be his most complete production role to date is not recognised as such by the public, *doesn't* release a second LP of Wailers tracks he has in the can in 1971. Instead, he gets on with innumerable other projects. Some of Perry's Wailers material sneaks out on various Trojan singles throughout 1971-2.

By 1973, Marley has signed to Island Records and starts drawing an unprecedented amount of attention. So Trojan put out the 'African Herbsman' LP of mostly Perry-produced material. Perry knows a good thing when he sees it, and releases 'Soul Revolution' on his Maroon label. But, the sleeve, which is blue with full-colour pictures, says 'Soul Revolution II'. By some twisted logic, Perry considered that 'Soul Rebels', even though it had a different title, was 'Soul Revolution Part 1'.

By 1973, the dub craze is starting to erupt, and Perry realises that he could make a quick killing with a Bob Marley dub LP, so he releases a version of 'Soul Revolution II' without the vocals. (If the record had been made any later, Perry would have made it a 'proper' dub LP with a remix, as he soon did with other material.) Perry presses it up on his Upsetter label, but, crucially, it's not the label circa 1971, with the writing going vertically down one side, it's the one circa 1973 with the writing squarely across the top. And on the label it says 'Soul Revolution II', credited to The Upsetter, *not* Bob Marley & The Wailers. In short, it could be given the same name as the vocal LP, because Perry considered it to be by a different artist – himself. Ironically, Tuff Gong distributed it.

So why the confusion over sleeves? Why has no Upsetters version of 'Soul Revolution II' cover turned up to confirm it? Because Perry's dub albums – 'Rhythm Shower', 'Blackboard Jungle', 'Cloak & Dagger' (original versions) – were *never* issued in sleeves. The confusion over sleeves, and which colour denotes the original pressing,

comes from the American Black Heart label, who made a cheap, single-colour-repro green copy of the Jamaican version of 'Soul Revolution II' for the vocal album, and many have assumed that his sleeve was the original Jamaican one. In fact, the original was the turquoise/full colour pictures one. Further confirmation comes from the sleeve shots, which feature The Wailers holding guns. Since the pictures were a few years old, and The Wailers had since out-grown their rude boy image, they castigated Perry for using such photographs: it would ruin the new hippieish collective persona that Island was promoting.

Just to confuse matters, Perry was also contemplating pressing a Trojan-style release as two albums with vocal tracks on one side and instrumentals on the other. Rumour has it that this was to be called 'Soul Revolution Rhythm Part III' and '...Part 4'. Labels may exist for the former, although only Trojan pressed the album in this format. They are now phenomenally hard to get, but were, until the following entry, the easiest way of getting the instrumental LP. The matrix number, TTL65/66, also suggests a date of circa 1973.

Track listing: as previous entry, minus the vocals.

BOB MARLEY & THE WAILERS: 'SOUL REVOLUTION I AND II'

TROJAN DOUBLE LP TRLD 406, 1988

The Soul Revolution vocal album, together with its instrumental counterpart, with four extra tracks. 'Soul Rebel' (as in the 'Soul Rebels' LP), 'Mr Brown' (reputedly the first Wailers/Perry collaboration of the era, a strange, thunderous song about a man in a coffin who frightened half of Kingston according to the *Gleaner* newspaper), also available on several Jamaican Upsetter 45 pressings, and on UK Upsetter and Trojan singles; and their 'dub' versions, 'Soul Rebel version 4', and 'Dracula'. The instrumental half of the album, ie 'Soul Revolution II', also forms part of Trojan's 'The Early Years 1969-73' box set.

BOB MARLEY & THE WAILERS: 'AFRICAN HERBSMAN'

TROJAN TRL 62, 1973. CDTRL 62, 1988

The 'Soul Revolution' album with the addition of tracks listed below.

The album also forms part of Trojan's 'The Early Years 1969-73' box set.

LIVELY UP YOURSELF

Bob's self-produced rabble-rouser, later to appear on the 'Natty Dread' and 'Live!' LPs. This 1971 prototype, a Tuff Gong production, was strong enough in itself, with great horns from Tommy McCook. Also a single on Trojan in the UK and Tuff Gong in Jamaica (1971), the latter with a version, 'Live' credited to Tommy McCook.

SMALL AXE

The classic attack on the 'big t'ree' producers in Jamaica and oppressors everywhere, with horns. Also released on UK (US 357, 1971) and Jamaican Upsetter 45s, and on 'The Very Best Of the Early Years 1968-74'. A later version appears on 'Burnin''. Another, Perry-produced, slower cut, minus horns, 'More Axe' appears on 'The Best Of Bob Marley and The Wailers' and 'The Very Best Of The Early Years 1968-74'.

DUPPY CONQUEROR

Bob's promise to ruin all those who try to spook him out, a duppy being a ghost. It wasn't the only song in reggae at the time on the same theme, with Prince Buster's 'Bull Buck (and Duppy Conqueror)' probably beating Bob to the punch. This is, however, the definitive statement on the subject. (Instrumental version on the 'Soul Revolution'/'Soul Revolution II' LPs, later recut for 'Catch A Fire'. Also a single on UK [US 348] & Jamaican Upsetter labels and, oddly, also appears on Trojan's 'Rasta Revolution' LP.) Produced by Lee Perry.

TRENCHTOWN ROCK
MARLEY

Another of Bob's fine shake-'em-up songs. A Tuff Gong JA/Green Door UK single as 'Trenchtown Rock', both with an instrumental version on the flip, and later on the 'Live!' LP. This cut is as stirring as any. Marley also put U Roy on the original backing track for a DJ cut called 'Kingston 12 Shuffle'. A Tuff Gong production.

ALL IN ONE

A medley of 'Bend Down Low', 'Nice Time', 'One Love', 'Simmer Down', 'It Hurts To Be Alone', 'Lonesome Feeling', 'Love And Affection', 'Put It On', 'Duppy Conqueror'. Bunny's & Peter's harmonies on 'It Hurts To Be Alone' are real heart-breakers. Also released on UK (US 357) and Jamaican Upsetter 7". The other Wailers medley is 'Rebel's Hop' ('Soul Rebels'/'Rasta Revolution' LPs).

BOB MARLEY & THE WAILERS: 'RASTA REVOLUTION'
TROJAN TRL 89, 1974; CDTRL 89, 1988

The 'Soul Rebels' album in a different running order, minus 'My Sympathy', and adding two tracks: 'Mr Brown' (details: 'Soul Revolution 1 & 2') and 'Duppy Conqueror' (see previous entry). Sleevenote by Lisa McAvoy. The album also forms part of Trojan's 'The Early Years 1969-73' LP.

ISLAND/TUFF GONG
PRODUCTIONS

THE WAILERS: CATCH A FIRE

ISLAND ILPS 9241, 4.5.73, REISSUED MANGO ILPM 9241 30.3.87; TUFF GONG TGLLP 1/CD
TGLCD 1, 26.11.90

After The Wailers' relationship with Lee Perry petered out, Marley spent some time working on singles for his own label, Tuff Gong. At some point in 1972 Chris Blackwell, the Anglo-Jamaican founder of Island Records, sought Marley out and offered him a verbal contract. Some pundits claim that Blackwell originally wanted to sign Toots & The Maytals and settled for Marley instead, although this seems unlikely since Blackwell had already produced Toots and therefore had all the opportunities he needed to strike any deal he wanted.

Blackwell gave £4,000 to The Wailers to make this album. They were now bolstered by The Upsetters' rhythm section of Carlie and Family Man Barrett, who had largely split with Perry, though both Bob and the Barrett brothers still worked with Perry occasionally throughout their career: nothing in Jamaican music is permanent. It also reputedly cost Island a payment to CBS, and to Danny Sims, who also had points on several Marley Island LPs. Although everyone in Jamaica reckoned that Blackwell would see

nothing for his money or Marley and Co. again, his faith was justified, and in 1973 The Wailers, now a full band, released 'Catch A Fire'.

Blackwell cleverly marketed The Wailers in the manner with which he had already achieved success for Island rock acts like Traffic, Cat Stevens and Fairport Convention. He presented them as an alternative to mainstream rock music, and doubtless their rebel image and Bob's growing locks, reminiscent to a white audience of the hippieish rock of the era, helped a lot. 'Catch A Fire' drew cautiously favourable, to ecstatic, if bewildered reviews from a UK music press that usually dismissed reggae as the province of skinheads (reggae review singles were forever available at bargain prices in London's secondhand stores) and Bob's was suddenly a name to drop for the campus hip. Island's marketing strategy had been very effective for their rock acts and the same style, ironically, would make a legend out of a singer famous in his own country for a decade, yet whom few white fans had heard of before 1973. Blackwell's company had tried to market reggae before with Jimmy Cliff, who nearly became a major star at the time of 'The Harder They Come' (1972) and had had a couple of huge chart hits in Britain ('Wonderful World, Beautiful People', 1969; 'Wild World', written by Cat Stevens, 1970).

The album was credited to The Wailers, which gives the lie to the common assertion that Island's insistence on Bob as the front man split the band. In truth, Marley's name had often been used out front (such as on the Lee Perry-produced LPs), just as Peter Tosh's had (on several singles). The brief explanatory sleeve note manages to spell Peter and Bunny's names incorrectly however (McIntosh was 'Mackintosh',

Livingston was 'Livingstone'). It's also the only reggae album to come in a flip-up sleeve shaped like a Zippo lighter! (The Jamaican issue wasn't shaped, neither were the reissues.) Recorded at Dynamic, Harry J, Randy's and Kingston Studios, with which The Wailers were already familiar, and mixed in London at Island's own suite in Basing Street, London, where overdubs also took place, with production credits going to Bob Marley and Chris Blackwell.

'Catch A Fire' was originally scheduled to come out as a rare LP on Island's Blue Mountain label, even given a suitable matrix, BML 2001, which appeared on the original stamper and was crossed off. This suggests that the project was to have been far more low-key than it subsequently became, even though the lone Wailers Blue Mountain single, 'Baby Baby We've Got A Date', garnered strong reviews in the UK music press, uniquely for a reggae single. At the time Blackwell had a loose plan to make Blue Mountain Island's reggae division, although the idea was soon dropped when he decided that The Wailers might catch on with a white audience if they were marketed just as strongly as a rock band. It took time, but he was undoubtedly correct.

The first Jamaican pressing, catalogue number 19329 FG, featured the same mixes as the UK version on a Tuff Gong label apparently never used elsewhere, featuring a dread bashing a gong. It is a commonly held belief that Jamaican pressings of Marley LPs featured different mixes. They did not, although sometimes the mastering process may have left the sound slightly amended from the original: this is more likely to be a muting, rather than an enhancing effect.

Band-members: Marley, Tosh, Livingston, Aston Barrett (bass), Carlton Barrett (drums). Various session players noted in details below. Also on the sessions: Earl 'Wire' Lindo, Tyrone Downie ('Stir It Up', 'Concrete Jungle'), Winston Wright, Glen Adams (kbds), Alva Lewis (guitar); Willy San Francisco, Winston Wright, Chris Karen (percussion); Rita Marley & Marcia Griffiths (backing vocals).

All songs: Bob Marley unless stated.

CONCRETE JUNGLE

Hey, guitar solos, like Roger McGuinn tuning up! A beat that doesn't reveal itself as reggae for a few bars. If you wanted to launch reggae on a rock audience that knows nothing about it, you do it like this. Although the mix is decidedly strange in places to reggae ears, it soon makes sense. And then, dammit, it's The Wailers. Sounding better-produced than ever before, more confident, and suddenly altogether more adult. Scan the credits, and Tosh's name says "guitar", but not lead. In fact it was Wayne Perkins, an American session musician, who put the licks on at Island's behest.

The other uncredited musician was John 'Rabbit' Bundrick, an erstwhile Free member who added keyboards and who was part of the Johnny Nash band when Marley was first in Europe in the early Seventies (see 'Acoustic Medley' on 'Songs Of Freedom', and 'Chances Are'). Exactly why these people were uncredited at the time is a mystery of marketing, but maybe Island felt it would be confusing to have both a Bunny and a Rabbit in the same group! The Wailers' thoughts on this at the time are unrecorded, although Marley later gave Perkins' work his approval and was reputedly present on at least one overdub date. The Jamaican session for 'Concrete Jungle' did not feature Family Man Barrett, a youth called Robbie Shakespeare taking the bass role. The song is a defining moment for Marley: here's the wise sufferer's stance in a nutshell.

It was a single on Island (WIP 6164, 1973), was collected onto 'Songs Of Freedom', and later appeared on 'Babylon By Bus'.

SLAVE DRIVER

Here's where the album title came from: "Slave driver, catch a fire so you can get burned". The fantastic harmonies Wailers fans have, by now, become used to, dominate this track, reinforced by a scratchy Tosh guitar. Bob's blood runs cold at the crack of a whip, which it must have done often since something akin to handclaps forms a whiplash whenever he mentions it. An instant classic, later covered in fine style by Dennis Brown (1977).

Also an Island single (WIP 6167, 1973), and appears on 'Songs Of Freedom' and 'Rebel Music'. A different version shows up on 'Talkin' Blues'.

400 YEARS
TOSH

Tosh retreads a track from the 'Soul Rebels' LP. Here the tempo is slower, and the attitude more laid-back and meandering, with a clavinet roaming around in the middle eight like a lost soul wandering the cosmos. The writing credit is still

Marley on the original label, although the sleeve has it as Tosh, which is more like the truth.

STOP THAT TRAIN
TOSH

Tosh again remakes an old song in a slower, gospellish style, this time a version of the track from 'The Best Of The Wailers'. Organ, credited to Tosh on the sleeve, sounds more like the work of a sessioner, and adds to the churchified atmosphere.

An instrumental cut of the song forms the flip to the UK single 'Baby Baby We've Got A Date' (1973), both on the Blue Mountain and later Island pressings. Tosh cut it yet again for the 'Mama Africa' album (1983).

BABY WE'VE GOT A DATE (ROCK IT BABY)

The Wailers first Island single (on the UK Blue Mountain (BM 1021) label as 'Baby Baby We've Got A Date', and on US Island as 'Rock It Baby', both 1973) of the new deal, also pressed for Tuff Gong as 'Rock It Babe'. Obtrusive slide guitar from Wayne Perkins again, and uncredited female vocals (Marcia Griffiths and Rita Marley, most likely) provide support for the sort of *let's get together baby* song you'd expect from their Leslie Kong period.

STIR IT UP

Another one from their rocksteady era remade. Johnny Nash had already had a hit with it (CBS, 1972) and this precise, neat version, with what sounds like more dubbed guitar, has an ease that Nash didn't achieve. Later to appear on the live 'Babylon By Bus' LP and a favourite of their first UK tour in 1973. Uncredited musicians also on the track: Ian & Roger Lewis (bass and guitar, both later in Inner Circle), Sparrow Martin (drums). Although the Barrett brothers were official bandmembers, Bob's musicians varied from day to day.

Unbelievably, considering its commercial potential, this version was not a 45 until 1976 and then not an A-side (WIP 6309 UK, IS 089 US).

KINKY REGGAE

'Kinky' was a bit of a catchword in early-70s Jamaica, appearing on a good few records. Bob uses the word here to mean a general sexiness. Lyrically, this is another precursor to 'Natty Dread', with Bob wandering through various areas describing the people he meets, and seemingly unable to decide whether he wants to live in a kinky part of town or not. The "Right on" chorus was also common in reggae at the time.

'Kinky Reggae' was also central to the live set of the time, and a steamy live cut later turned up on the 'Talkin' Blues' set (1991), as well as 'Babylon By Bus' (1978) and as the flip to 'No Woman No Cry' (1975 on UK single drawn from the same shows that produced the breakthrough 'Live!' set). The song has an unselfconscious air that became increasingly rare as Bob's fame grew.

NO MORE TROUBLE

Bob, clavinet and more uncredited female vocals, rejects problems to a bassline reminiscent of Isaac Hayes' 'Do Your Thing', another reggae cover-version favourite. Carlie Barrett's 'one drop' drum style is particularly magnificent here, otherwise this slight song is the least-interesting thing on the album.

This version also appears on US 45 (Island 1215) and the 'Songs Of Freedom' set. A live cut, segued into 'War', turns up on 'Babylon By Bus' and 'Rebel Music'.

MIDNIGHT RAVERS

A rootsy one to close the album with the sort of

raw mix usually found on Tuff Gong 45 rather than album. As indeed it was (1972), with a magnificent instrumental version with a strange flanged mix (which tips over into feedback) for the flip. Glorious harmonies on this version, and the apocalyptic vision of confused sexes and 10,000 horseless chariots must have seemed baffling to first-time Marley buyers not used to his Book Of Revelations imagery. A remarkable record any way you look at it.

THE WAILERS: 'BURNIN''

ILPS 9256 19.10.73; REISSUE MANGO ILPM 9256 30.3.87; TUFF GONG TGLLP 2, CD TGLCD 2 26.11.90

Having caused a fuss in the white media far beyond most reggae album standards with 'Catch A Fire', the logical step was 'Burnin'', with a title that recalls a predecessor released in the same year. A more focused, less cautious album than 'Catch A Fire', it featured The Wailers, now expanded to a six-piece with the addition of Earl 'Wire' Lindo on keyboards, on the front cover, while a fresh brand burns the title into the wood of a crate – the sort of crate and brand used on slaves. The rear sleeve has Bob pulling on a long spliff, implying freedom. The gatefold sleeve gave us the lyrics and a set of idyllic-looking photographs of Jamaican ghetto life, showing poverty in a positive light. There had been gatefold reggae sleeves before – The Upsetters' 'Return Of Django', for example – but nothing in the genre had looked as perfect for a wider audience than this to date.

Recorded at Harry J, Kingston, and once again mixed at Island, London, the album was well-received by the rock press, but despite encouraging sales and shows in England (including a TV appearance on *The Old Grey Whistle Test*), it wasn't the commercial breakthrough band and label hoped for. It was, however, another rung on the ladder, and following within six months of 'Catch A Fire', 'Burnin'' made it plain that here was a prolific talent. It also showed Bunny getting involved – for the last time – after its predecessor's Bunny-free song catalogue.

Produced by Chris Blackwell & The Wailers. All songs by Bob Marley unless stated.

Musicians: Marley, Tosh, Livingston, A & C Barrett, Earl Lindo. Other musicians: Tyrone Downie, keyboards.

GET UP, STAND UP
MARLEY/TOSH

Perhaps more confident of what they had, there is no mystery about what sort of record 'Burnin'' would turn out to be from the first notes of the LP. Marley and Tosh, in an almost unique writing-credit job-share scheme, turn out a tune largely fronted by Bob but with a message that seems almost entirely Tosh's in its militancy and attitude. Tosh's vocal on the final verse was never bettered: here he was singing with a confidence that hadn't seemed so plain since the mid-Sixties. Something of an anthem, it gave the sentiment of their earlier single 'Lively Up Yourself' an altogether more fierce edge.

The song was also an Island 45 coupled with 'Slave Driver' (WIP 6167 UK, P 1218 promo only US), it was collected onto 'Rebel Music' and 'Songs Of Freedom', there's a cut on 'Live!', and a different version appears on the 'Talkin' Blues' album.

HALLELUJAH TIME
JEAN WATT

A sure sign that Bunny's impending departure from the group was inevitable, no matter what the true reasons were (a dislike of touring, and a fear of being in Bob's shadow are often mooted). Credited to Jean Watt, Bunny's wife, 'Hallelujah Time' is a far gentler, more spiritual song than the rest of the material here, more in keeping with Bunny's own début album, 'Blackheart Man' (1976) than 'Burnin''. Bunny examines Rasta and

humanity through the the works of nature and the evils of slavery.

I SHOT THE SHERIFF

The song that 'made' Bob for the music business, in that it became a US No 1 for Eric Clapton. The fact that Bob had already written hits for Johnny Nash counted for little, since Clapton was perceived as a serious artist, while Nash was supposedly just an occasional hitmaker. Needless to say, Bob's is the superior version, albeit not so dissimilar to Clapton's. The Wailers' harmonies here are slightly shriller than usual, suggesting that it might not be Bunny & Peter together.

The song, controversial in Jamaica at the time, was, according to Bob, meant to be 'I Shot The Police' but Bob chose the Wild West motif to avoid trouble. It has a repeated ability to put the law's nose out of joint: it was banned from all public performance in Jamaica by the head of security in August 1993. For the probable inspiration behind the song, see 'Keep On Moving' on the 'Soul Revolution' LP.

The song also turned up on 'Live!' (1975), and Bunny returned to it on his 'Tribute' LP (1981/1990). It was also a hit for British funk band Light Of The World in 1981.

BURNIN' AND LOOTIN'

Another militant classic, downbeat, tough and penetrating. Bob wakes up in a curfew (curfews are regularly called in Kingston following bouts of violence or demonstrations) and takes the standpoint whereby the poor can't get to those who can help them, so force must be used. Bob later claimed that it was simply about burning mental illusions, and though that forms part of the lyric, it seems a disingenuous claim made at a time when Bob was under fire in Jamaica for 'going political'. Musically similar to 'Midnight Ravers', and Bob, incidentally, is part of the harmony team as well as singing lead. The song later appeared on 'Live!' and 'Talkin' Blues' in different forms.

PUT IT ON

The Studio One spiritual that opens 'The Wailing Wailers' given a tender, unfussy rework. Certainly not the best version, but some way short of being perfunctory. The song was also a single on Studio One and Island in its original form, and there's another cut on the 'Soul Revolution' LP.

SMALL AXE

Another oldie dusted down and remade, this time with a more inspired, chugging feel to it, and what sounds like a female voice amongst the harmonies, perhaps Marcia Griffiths'.

One of the most famous Wailers songs in its first incarnation, to be found as an Upsetter 45, on the 'Rasta Revolution' (QV) and 'Very Best Of The Early Years' LP, and in different form as 'More Axe' on the latter, which also, just to make life more complicated, came on 'The Best Of Bob Marley & The Wailers' as 'Small Axe'. Unusually, considering its classic status, there were no further versions made. Perhaps Bob had had enough of it by the time this cut was released.

PASS IT ON
JEAN WATT

Another Bunny Wailer-led song. With its almost-funky bassline and tinkling electric piano, at the start 'Pass It On' sounds like an American soul tune, something that a Bill Withers of the time might have put together. However, the Rasta drumming and folksy Jamaican style soon takes a grip. As with 'Hallelujah Time', 'Pass It On' is again at odds with much of the rest of the LP, being concerned with matters more spiritual than polemical. Bunny also cut a fine version as a single on his Solomonic label (1973, also appearing on the US Nighthawk label's 'Knotty Vision' LP), and there's a magnificent rocksteady original circa 1967/8 in the Tuff Gong vaults that has never seen the light of day.

DUPPY CONQUEROR

By now 'Burnin'' has shaken off the attacking nature of most of Side one and is gradually becoming more downbeat, as this reappraisal of another of their hits with Lee Perry testifies. Pretty much the same as the original, without the sense of urgency and with the backing vocals taking a more prominent part. The "Brrr" trills on the "Don't try to cold me out on this bridge" middle eight remain one of the most interesting wordplays concocted in reggae: not only is Bob talking about a physical bridge, but also a musical one, and the "Brrr" for "cold me out" adds another layer of meaning that takes a while to sink in.

The original came on the 'Soul Revolution' album in dub form and on 'African Herbsman' as a vocal, as well as on a variety of single releases (UK Upsetter US 348, several Jamaican pressings). There is also a DJ version of the original by Dave Barker as 'Conqueror v/3' (JA Upsetter), also pressed as just 'Duppy Conqueror' and as 'Runaway Child' (UK Upsetter US 349).

ONE FOUNDATION
TOSH

Tosh, with clavinet, wah-ing guitars and a bit of harpsichord to lead him in, emphasises the need for unity in a song that perhaps owes something to 'One Love', in sentiment if not in style. The Wailers' harmonies were never lusher than this, and never would be again since 'Burnin'' is the last time they'd be together for an entire LP. Unusually for him, Tosh never did the song again.

RASTA MAN CHANT
TRAD. ARRANGED WAILERS

The Wailers, with Rasta drums, hold a 'grounation' in the studio, chanting a spiritual that still echoes down from the Rasta encampments to this day. Another highlight of their early tours, it was pressed on a single Tuff Gong label as 'Chant I'. Who first wrote it is anyone's guess. Another version appears on the 'Talkin' Blues' album. Their harmonies never sounded better than they did here, and the moog solo, which, incredibly, manages to sound as natural as a bee buzzing overhead, is inspired. A fitting, delicious finale to The Wailers' career as a harmony group.

Also on 'Songs Of Freedom', and another cut appears on 'Talkin' Blues'.

BOB MARLEY & THE WAILERS: 'NATTY DREAD'

ISLAND ILPS 9281 25.10.74; REISSUES: MANGO ILPM 9281, CD CID 9281 30.3.87; TUFF GONG
TGLLP 3, CD TGLCD 3 26.11.90

1974, and Bob is now officially a solo artist for the first time since his début couple of sin-gles for Leslie Kong back in 1963. Shorn of the vocal support of Bunny and Peter, both of whom went off to launch or relaunch solo careers without Bob's shadow looming over them, Bob enlists the help of Rita Marley, his wife and former leader of female harmony group The Soulettes. They had supported Lee Perry on a few of his solo singles as well as cutting several records for Studio One when The Wailers were among the label's leading lights. Rita had also worked with The Wailers on innumerable occasions. Rita enlisted the help of Marcia Griffiths, a solo reggae star from the mid-60s and her work at Studio One, and former partner of Bob Andy in Bob & Marcia, who had a number one hit in the UK with a version of Nina Simone's 'Young, Gifted & Black'. Ironically, their other UK chart hit was 'Pied Piper', a Crispian St Peters song which Rita Marley had cut as her first solo release in 1966. The other member of the I-Threes was Judy Mowatt, formerly leader of The Gaylettes, who recorded extensively for producer Sonia Pottinger's Gay Feet label in the late-60s/early 70s. The change of backing vocalists left Bob right out front, while The I-Threes, no match for The Wailers in harmony sound, but not pretending to be, provided support and comment, strengthening rather than sweetening the melody.

The band had also been strengthened. Alongside Marley's rhythm guitar and The Barrett Brothers' bass and drums were Touter, (Bernard Harvey) on keyboards, and Al Anderson's lead guitar.

'Natty Dread', far from showing Bob nervous in his new working situation, cast him in his best light. The band get full credits on the album, even if The I-Threes just take a collective nod and the occasional session contribution goes unrecord-ed. Once again the album was recorded in Jamaica – at Harry J Studios, and mixed in London at Basing Street Studios. Producers are

Chris Blackwell and Bob Marley. The engineering credits are revealing: in Jamaica, Syl Morris, for some the best engineer Jamaica has produced, had worked at Studio One during the Sixties. So had Sid Bucknor, who handled the mix in England. This perhaps explained the natural affinity with Marley's music shown by both engineers. However, for the first time, Marley also recorded some of the backing tracks in London, at Island's Studios in Hammersmith: these tracks do not stand out from the rest in any way.

While once again not a huge commercial breakthrough, it was undoubtedly several steps in the right direction and 'Natty Dread' appeared briefly in the UK album chart for five weeks, peaking at 43. Bob's image was now up-front, as was his name. In England and America, the record gradually became *de rigueur* amongst the campus crowd, and by the time Bob's next album arrived, would spread even further. Despite the inevitable presence of three older songs – 'Lively Up Yourself', 'Bend Down Low' and 'Them Belly Full (But We Hungry)' – 'Natty Dread' seemed to look to the future, not the past. An undoubted artistic triumph, it is a must-have record for all Marley fans. However, it seems that while this is the definitive version of the album, there were others: as the LP was being mixed in London, provisional mixes of certain songs were put onto acetate, including some half a dozen alternate mixes of 'Natty Dread' itself, and are now in the hands of a sound-system owner in London.

Producer: Chris Blackwell & The Wailers. NB: this credit may indicate that Island were originally keen to maintain the collective band title rather than push Bob's name out front.

Musicians: Bob Marley (vcls, gtr); Aston Barrett (bass); Carlton Barrett (drums); Bernard 'Touter' Harvey (keyboards); Al Anderson (lead guitar). The I-Threes, Rita Marley, Marcia Griffiths, Judy Mowatt, (backing vocals). Also on the sessions: Earl 'Wire' Lindo, Tyrone Downie (kbds); Glen Da Costa, David Madden, Tommy McCook (horns).

LIVELY UP YOURSELF
MARLEY

If you weren't a Marley fan you could be forgiven for assuming that this is the first version of 'Lively Up Yourself', so fresh is it, unlike one or two of his other remakes. Littered with nylon-strung acoustic guitar licks from Al Anderson, and with a cool, light one-drop from Carlie Barrett, Bob makes light of his and the world's troubles and urges one and all to "don't be no drag". It's as urgent an appeal for involvement as an opener as was "Get Up, Stand Up' on 'Burnin'", but without the militancy.

The original single, on Tuff Gong (1971), also had Tommy McCook in charge of the horn section. That version can be found on the 'African Herbsman' LP. This version was a US single on Island (IS 027). The song later turned up on the 'Live!' album, and the 'Babylon By Bus' double-set, the only song to grace both official in-concert LPs. It's also one of the 'Songs Of Freedom'.

NO WOMAN, NO CRY
VINCENT FORD

Although reggae traditionalists complained about the arrival of the drum machine in the music in the mid-Eighties, complaining that the feel a drummer like Carlie Barrett could invest in a track would be lost, Carlie, Family Man and Marley were experimenting with an electronic sticksman back in the mid-Seventies. Here's the proof.

One of the all-time *rock* classics, never mind reggae or Marley classics, 'No Woman No Cry' in this form is treated with a far less anthemic approach than the hit version from the 'Live!' LP.

Instead, it's a slightly thin-sounding, tender treatment, short on skank and high on spirit, as Bob recalls the suffering of his past as a comfort for the present and future. While there's no doubting the sincerity of his tone, it might not specifically be his past at all: the writing credit is Vincent Ford.

There are several possible reasons for this. The first is that it was written by Vincent Ford, a paraplegic diabetic who to this day can be found hanging out around the Bob Marley Museum which was once the singer's home and studio at 56 Hope Road, Kingston. While there is no concrete reason to doubt that Ford was the author, some Marleyphiles suggest that it sounds like a Marley song, and anyway, if Ford wrote an absolute classic like this, why are his other contributions to music so scant as to be invisible? No, they argue, there are two possible reasons to doubt the authorship of the song: one is that Bob was signed at the time in a publishing deal with Cayman Music, a company owned by Danny Sims, Johnny Nash's manager. Bob had split with Sims, who was acting as his manager, in 1972, and perhaps resented his involvement in the singer's affairs. So, rather than Sims getting the publishing, Bob's own company, Bob Marley

BOB MARLEY & THE WAILERS 'NATTY DREAD'

Music, could get the royalties if someone else got the credit. They also point out that a fair few of the other songs on the album also have credits other than "Bob Marley" to support the argument.

The other reason is that Bob wanted to look after Ford financially, since he had been Bob's friend from the days when, as the lyric suggests, they had lived in Trenchtown. Since Ford had little hope of finding work because of his condition, it was the best way Bob could think of to take care of him. However, since Bob had no way of knowing that the song would become a classic and, as a result, accrue a fortune in royalties, he was acting very optimistically to assume that this gesture would take care of his friend. The simplest explanation is that Ford wrote the lyrics, or at least sang them, while Bob was strumming out in the yard of Hope Road one day. Both Ford and his son, a frequent visitor to Bob's Tuff Gong premises today, are adamant that the song is as credited, and why shouldn't he have written it?

The alternative argument is that Bob, now without Bunny & Peter to bounce ideas off, was seeking support from elsewhere, and that 'Natty Dread', with its air of collective good living, reflects that. Hence even Vincent Ford, with no

known musical history, might have penned an unarguable classic under the Tuff Gong régime of all pulling together for the greater good. If that is the truth of the matter, it fits Marley's image of the time perfectly.

Also an Island 45 in the version to be found on 'Live!' There's a different in-concert cut on 'Songs Of Freedom'.

THEM BELLY FULL (BUT WE HUNGRY)
MARLEY

Previously released as both 'Bellyfull' and 'Belly Full' on Tuff Gong 7" singles in marginally different versions, this cut of Bob's song about physical and spiritual hunger retains much of the rootsiness of the earlier pressings through its use of a horn section on the guitar 'chucks'. The lyrics can be read two ways: the "them" of the title might be the rich, the oppressors, or it might be that you can have a full belly but not a full soul. The theme of the chorus is one that still occurs in reggae: "Forget your weakness and dance, forget your sickness and dance." Here is reggae as mender of broken spirits.

Bob also did the song on the 'Live!' album. It's also on 'Rebel Music'.

REBEL MUSIC (THREE O'CLOCK ROADBLOCK)
ASTON BARRETT, HUGH PEART

Emphasising reggae's place as a music of the Jamaican poor, a role it still plays today even if it's not Bob's music that performs it, 'Rebel Music' presents a picture of a Rasta – musician? – stopped by the police in a land where everyone is free in theory. Bob's play-acting between the police and Rasta, culminating in "I ain't got no birth cerificate on me now," is masterly. He knew that it wasn't the 'correct' way to say certificate, but as in the real situation, he was emphasising the difference between his standards and the cops', putting a distance between them. Set to a crunching skank, and with Lee Jaffe's (uncredited) harmonica wailing like a fox howling in the dead of night, 'Rebel Music' takes the concept that first arrived with 'Soul Rebels' into another dimension.

The song also turned up on the 'Babylon By Bus' LP, and was a single in Jamaica on Tuff Gong as '3 O'Clock Road Block' (1974) with a harmonica mix, 'Rebel Music', on the other side. It gave a title and an opening track to 'Rebel Music'.

SO JAH SEH
WILLIE SAN FRANCISCO

Bob unleashes his Rasta consciousness in a way that he hadn't done on record too often in the past few years. Divining his place in the broader scheme of things, Bob offers the word of God as proof that his kids, and by extension, the other children of the poor, shall not starve for want of the monied classes' charity. Once again a popping drum machine takes precedence over a live kit, and set against a tight, dry horn section and the light, skipping melody, it's an effective device and renders the song one of Bob's most complex to date. Once again we have the problem of who actually wrote the song: credit here is Willie San Francisco (Francisco Willy Pep), part of Bob's posse, often playing percussion.

The track also came as a single (Island WIP 6262, 1974) with 'Natty Dread' as a flip. It was also the US reverse of 'Lively Up Yourself' (IS 027, 1974).

NATTY DREAD
ALAN COLE/ASTON BARRETT

And so the classics keep coming. Bob moves from street to street, hearing the kids shouting "Natty dread!" at him, which he does not take as an insult, but merely a statement of glorious fact. Lyrically slight, but nonetheless making its point, Bob appears to be freestyling through the tune, making occasional cultural points before reaching a simple climax that states just how far he is from his real spiritual home, Africa. However, the self-assured, solid performance makes the song far more than it superficially appears to be.

It was also a single in Jamaica as 'Knotty Dread' with a dub version on the reverse (Tuff Gong, 1974), and the vocal and mix is different here. The authors of the song according to the credit are Alan 'Skill' Cole, Bob's footballer buddy, and Family Man. In fact, if you listen closely to the album version, you can hear a bit of the discarded vocal towards the end of the track. It was also issued on the B-side of 'So Jah Seh' (Island WIP 6262). In concept, the song bears a considerable resemblance to 'Soul Rebel' (from the 'Soul Rebels' album), and interestingly, to 'Bongo Red', a single from leading Seventies roots reggae band The Gladiators. (Oddly, certain reissue pressings of 'Bongo Red' date its original release as August 1974, virtually claiming The Wailing Souls' idea as the original concept. But since their record was on Studio One, maybe the label-owner, Coxsone Dodd, was just having

a little dig at his former protégé.) Also issued on UK Island 45 (WIP 6262) and on 'Songs Of Freedom'.

BEND DOWN LOW
MARLEY

Bob returns to rocksteady days for another look at one of his more enduring Sixties hits. Despite the countryish guitars on the opening, this is recognisably the same song and virtually the same arrangement, even if the I-Threes' harmonies are more bluesy than The Wailers'. Bob remembers his sassy, rude past as he was wont to do on occasion during his years as an international star. The organ solo in the middle recalls yet another reggae era, circa 1969-70 in its reedy, thin tone. The slightest thing on the album, and probably inferior to the original (to be found on 'The Best Of The Wailers' and 'One Love') but a necessary lightener on a side packed with messages. Rumour has it that this natural single release was deemed too lightweight for Bob's growing serious artist image.

TALKIN' BLUES
CARLTON BARRETT/L COGILL

Another song with a rock-solid skank behind it

like 'Them Belly Full', while Bob, with Lee Jaffe's harmonica again wailing the blues in the background, depicts himself as a sufferer, no roof over his head and rocks for his pillow. This is, apparently, no accident, since his position as a Rasta, made clear by his "Feel like bombing a church, now that you know that the preacher is lying" middle-eight, would be likely to render him unemployable. That line earned the song a considerable controversial reputation, and maybe, just maybe, Bob doesn't feel so confident singing it on close listening. The song is also partly about gossip. A final point: the last verse's vocals may have been cut at a different time, or have been edited in later, since Bob's voice changes considerably in timbre as it comes in. This track was a UK single (WIP 6262).

A different version of the song also appears on, and gives the title to, the 'Talking Blues' LP. There's also a Tuff Gong single (1974) that also features a toast from I Roy with Bob's vocal, with a dub mix on the reverse.

REVOLUTION
MARLEY

A slow chunky skank, with Rasta drumming rattling about somewhere in the middle of the mix,

closes the album. The chord changes have a steady inevitability about them, and the compressed-sounding horn lines, similar to those later used on Dennis Brown's 'Life's Worth Living' (Dennis was reputedly Bob's favourite reggae singer), give the song a real atmosphere and bite. Doubtless its lyrical content was partly influenced by Niney's 'Blood And Fire', a record that Bob was more than aware of since he had a much-publicised argument about it when it was released in 1970. If Bob's voice has a faintly affected twang about it as he calls for an uprising, be it bloody or apocalyptic, there's a true air of finality about the song which suits its position as album-closer down to the ground.

BOB MARLEY & THE WAILERS; 'A TASTE OF THE WAILERS'
ISLAND PROMO-ONLY LP ISS 3, MAY 1975

Designed to set the scene for the tour that produced the 'Live!' set, this album was issued in the UK only for press and radio promotional purposes in limited quantities. There was no sleeve as such, just a rubber-stamp title on a white card cover. Details as on previous Island LPs.

Tracks: 'Lively Up Yourself', 'Kinky Reggae', 'No Woman No Cry', 'Get Up Stand Up', 'I Shot The Sheriff', 'Stir It Up', 'Natty Dread'.

BOB MARLEY & THE WAILERS: 'LIVE!' AKA 'LIVE AT THE LYCEUM'

ISLAND ILPS 9376 5.12.'75; REISSUES: MANGO ILPM 9376 30.3.87; CD CID 9376 19.1.87; TUFF GONG TGLLP 4, CD TGLCD 4 26.11.90

A t last, the international commercial breakthrough, in Europe at least. Greeted with a bunch of reviews that stressed 'Live!''s instant-classic status, the album catapulted Bob from man-most-likely-to status to stardom. It took time in the States, however, since Island, inexplicably, didn't release it there immediately, perhaps trying to build a buzz on import. When it did come out, the rock radio stations, rather than the black ones, played it regularly.

In an era when the strength of live performance mattered above all else, it was a masterstroke for Bob and Island to capture his dynamite show on wax. If Bob could make a great in-concert record, what could hold him back?

Recorded at London's now-defunct Lyceum Theatre on The Rolling Stones' Mobile on July 18, 1975, it was a document of a celebratory night, a must-attend gig for fans of mid-Seventies reggae. Bob had been here before, but this was the first time he had drawn a crowd like this. There had been live reggae albums before, but here was the first time a Jamaican performer of his magnitude had committed it on wax. 'Live!' was a faithful live document, rough,

and buzzing with the electricity of the moment, as if everyone concerned, from crowd to live engineer to The Barrett Brothers' peerless rhythm section, knew Bob's time had finally come. The mix is hardly like the studio reggae of the time, but why should it be? Bob was taking the sound to new ears without preconceptions. There are no announcements from Bob, and just one, at the start of the record, from entourage-member Tony 'T' Garnett.

Credits read as follows: "Bob Marley & The Wailers produced the music. Steve Smith & Chris Blackwell produced the record." The record produced a star.

Musicians: Bob Marley, Aston & Carlton

Barrett, Bernard Touter Harvey, Al Anderson. The I-Threes minus one (I-Twos?): Judy Mowatt was not on the tour.

The actual set-list for the gig was as follows: Intro; 'Trenchtown Rock', 'Slave Driver', 'Burnin' And Lootin', 'Them Belly Full (But We Hungry)', 'Three O'Clock Roadblock', 'No Woman, No Cry', 'Kinky Reggae', 'Natty Dread', 'Stir It Up', 'Lively Up Yourself', 'I Shot The Sheriff', 'Get Up, Stand Up'.

TRENCHTOWN ROCK
MARLEY

A rough, high-stepping cut of the song from 'African Herbsman'/'Natty Dread'. You can feel the buzz in band and crowd alike. The I-not-quite-Threes' harmonies are as raw as Bob's lead. Left remarkably messy in the mix, with no sign of a later overdub fix, the purr of the crowd is such in places that you could imagine Bob playing within the audience rather than onstage. And that was, by all accounts, what it felt like.

BURNIN' & LOOTIN'
MARLEY

Although largely faithful to the version on 'Burnin'', 'Burnin' & Lootin'' here displays a punchy, ragged edge, elevating Bob to the first gurgling, trance-like improvisations of the night. Although the sense of a party for the minority who knew of Bob's magic remains, the performance invests enough gravitas into the song to render its message unmistakable.

THEM BELLY FULL
L COGILL/C BARRETT

Another message song, this time from 'Natty Dread', delivered in a tight, faithful fashion, with Bob extending himself towards the end in a manner that would become familiar to all who saw him live from this point on, repeating lines over and over to a careful response from the backing singers. While this rendition lacks the anger of the studio versions, it gains a kind of determined other-worldliness as singer and band get into the groove of it as it progresses.

LIVELY UP YOURSELF
MARLEY

Getting the biggest greeting from the crowd so far, making it plain that the song was, in fact, the last on the night before the encores, rather than midway through the set as the running order of the LP suggests, is Bob's classic demand for a display of commitment. Nowhere near as impressive a performance as the studio versions, but as a rabble-rouser, with an energy that apparently cannot be held in check by a band that was often metronomically accurate, speeding up towards the end, you can't ask for more. Bob's apparent disappearance towards the end does not hamper the conclusion in any manner.

NO WOMAN, NO CRY
V FORD

The hit. No 'No Woman, No Cry', no record collection. Riding on Touter's superior organ, this full-length cut remains one of the most emotive pieces of music put on record, and although the first version on 'Natty Dread' is in itself wondrous, the sheer grace and majesty of this live cut is unsurpassed.

A different live cut appears on 'Songs Of Freedom'. Single: WIP 6244 UK, IS 037 US. There's also a 12" pressing of the former.

I SHOT THE SHERIFF
MARLEY

Set to a light, swinging skank that is the opposite of the tight, dry version on 'Burnin'', 'I Shot The Sheriff' gains new life as part of a live performance. Stretched out a little, with a piano solo from Touter towards the end, the almost casual manner with which The Wailers knock this one out betrays the massive dignity and rebellion of the song: how can they sound this relaxed and yet retain the militancy? But somehow they do, and 'Sheriff' is all the better for it. This version also appears on the 'Songs Of Freedom' set. The version from the other night of the two they played at the Lyceum is on the 'Talkin' Blues' LP.

GET UP, STAND UP
MARLEY/TOSH

The only nod to Tosh on the LP is another easy bit of militancy. Bob handles Peter's verses in a manner that is largely his own, never offering the anger of Tosh, instead preferring a matter-of-fact tone that makes it seem that the fight that you "don't give up" is one that is just a part of life rather than a burst of fury. The "Woy-oh!" chants at the end later found their way onto 'Punky Reggae Party', Bob's tribute to 'new wave' rock. As the vamping chorus from The I-Threes fades out at the end, you realise that you have been part of a great event in modern music.

BOB MARLEY & THE WAILERS: 'RASTAMAN VIBRATION'
ISLAND ILPS 9383 30.4.76; REISSUES: MANGO ILPM 9383, CD CID 9383 30.3.87;
TUFF GONG TGLLP/CD 5 26.11.90

Having achieved a considerable coup with 'Live!', Bob returned to the studio for his next album, full of songs that would be entirely new to his now-burgeoning white audience, even if some were familiar to Jamaican listeners. The spirit of the album was very different from that of 'Natty Dread', the previous studio set, less upbeat and more mellow. For some, the record was something of a disappointment after the sheer excitement and energy of its predecessors, but none the less there are moments here that stand with anything in the Marley canon, the closing tracks 'War' and 'Rat Race' in particular. Bob was not rocking out like he had done before, instead preferring a reflective tone on 'Johnny Was', 'Cry To Me' and 'Positive Vibration'.

Recorded at Harry J and Joe Gibbs' studios in Kingston with engineers Sylvan Morris and Errol 'T' Thompson, and mixed at Criteria, Miami by Aston Barrett and Chris Blackwell, 'Rastaman Vibration' was the first of Marley's albums simply given the credit "Produced by Bob Marley & The Wailers".

Musicians: Marley, Ashton & Carlton Barrett, Tyrone Downie, The I Threes; Alvin 'Seeco' Petterson (percussion), Earl 'Chinna' Smith, Donald Kinsey, Al Anderson (guitars); Tommy McCook, Glen da Costa, David Madden (horns).

POSITIVE VIBRATION
V FORD

A slurring, unhurried Bob outlines a message remarkably similar to that of the positivity-touting rappers of the late Eighties, declaring arguments to be prayers to the devil. With a noodly, lazy Moog beneath the vocals, a drumbeat reduced to an almost inaudible hi-hat and heavy bass-drum bolstered with crunching hand-drums, this is a decidedly downbeat way to open an album, and almost the musical antithesis to the title. Hardly the ideal album-opener after the brightness of 'Natty Dread', there's little real depth here. Both it, and the next track, have a writing credit of "V Ford", ie Vincent Ford of 'No Woman No Cry' (see 'Natty Dread' LP). It was a UK single (WIP 26348).

ROOTS, ROCK, REGGAE
V FORD

Utilising a lyric that Bob also used as 'Rainbow Country' ('The Upsetter Record Shop Part II' LP), 'Roots, Rock, Reggae' is almost an appeal to the American music business, with the words "Play I on the R&B", meaning make me part of US black radio programming, appearing several times. It is as slight as such songs usually are.

Also appeared on UK & US Island (WIP 26348, WIP 6309; IS 060, 072) and Jamaican Tuff Gong singles.

JOHNNY WAS
R MARLEY

Credited to R Marley (Rita), as opposed to Bob Marley, who gets the credit only on 'Cry To Me' and 'Night Shift', both older songs that Bob could hardly deny writing, implying further escape from the Cayman music contract. 'Johnny Was' offers a lyric about a son's death so stark as to be brutal. The story is that a Jamaican ghetto rudie is shot in the street, leaving his mum wondering where she went wrong. "Wondering how she can work it out now that she knows that the wages of sin is death, the gift of Jah is life," wails Bob, the clear implication being that had the kid been brought up a Rasta none of this need have happened. The chord structure returns to that of Bob's R&B days, and is somewhat similar to that of 'I'm Still Waiting' (see 'The Wailing Wailers' LP) for the end of the song. The lyric offers a fundamentalist approach to Bob's Rasta beliefs that may offend some, but was certainly a part of his never-straightforward personality. Musically, the song is interesting for its flanged effects and drum machine. Everyone says that the Johnny in question is Carlton 'Bat Man' Wilson, brother of singer Delroy and a rudie forced to retire after gunshot injury. Evidence to corroborate this tale is hard to find.

Also on the 'Songs Of Freedom' set, and appeared on UK 7" (WIP 6296).

CRY TO ME
MARLEY

More echoes of Bob's mid-Sixties era, this time with a straightforward cover of the 1966 Wailers song (see 'The Best Of The Wailers'). It was never the most compelling of Bob's songs, and without the harmonies of Bunny & Peter, replaced by a somewhat overbearing I-Threes', it sounds distinctly lame here. Perhaps Bob was suffering from a song-shortage at the time, although there are certainly better tunes in his past that he might have returned to. This, like 'Positive Vibration', sounds almost as if Bob was simply cutting songs in the studio without particularly intending release.

Also on UK & US 7" (WIP 6296/IS 060).

WANT MORE
ASTON BARRETT

This slow, downbeat one-drop examines greed and jealousy. The bassy, maudlin tone makes it one of the grimmer Marley performances, although enlivened by an urgent vocal. The song itself gradually drops away towards the end, giving way to what is almost a bass and drums dub version not dissimilar to the minimalist productions of the 'Soul Rebels' album. There are also some noteworthy bluesy guitar licks from Donald Kinsey to look out for lingering unobtrusively in the mix. .

CRAZY BALDHEAD
R MARLEY

With a banshee wail, the album suddenly improves for Side two of the vinyl pressing. Here is Bob as militant, non-Rasta hunter, on a song also rendered by Johnny Clarke (1977) in a cover perhaps even better-remembered in the reggae world than the original (another song credited to Rita). It is not, however, an entirely new song: much of the verses come from 'Freedom Time', the early (1967) self-produced single that remains one of the most eloquent and uplifting Marley performances. The "Chase those crazy bunk-beds" line refers to the presence of the military on Jamaica's streets. Something of an anthem, various boxers have used it to make their entrance more imposing.

Also on 'Rebel Music' and 'Songs Of Freedom'.

WHO THE CAP FIT
A BARRETT/C BARRETT

Another look over the shoulder: 'Who The Cap Fit' is a remake of an obscure Wailers single for the Upsetter label, 'Man To Man' (1971). Despite some severely dated synth-string sounds, this is a considerable improvement on the previous direct cover on the LP, 'Cry To Me', simply because The I-Threes harmonies are kept in exactly the right proportions to the main vocal, and the easy, laconic approach is almost identical to that of the original version, on which the Barrett brothers also played, presumably, and who get the writing credits for this cut. Came on a US 45 (IS 072).

Also on 'Songs Of Freedom'.

NIGHT SHIFT
MARLEY

A remake of 'It's Alright' (from 'Soul Rebels'), and far less successful than 'Who The Cap Fits' as a self-cover. The original was a funky, sparse thing, this version is a plodding, somewhat tedious skank. The song, casting Bob as a forklift driver, probably refers to the time he spent working nights at the Chrysler motor plant in Delaware, USA (1966), combined with a warehouse job operating a fork-lift which he took in the city.

WAR
A COLE/C BARRETT

The second unarguable Marley classic of the LP, 'War' draws its lyric (despite a writing credit of Alan 'Skill' Cole, the Jamaican footballer, and Carlie Barrett, Bob's drummer) from Emperor Haile Selassie's speech to the UN in 1968. Lacking the fire of Bob's live versions, it was, nonetheless, a song that Bob felt strongly enough about for it to become an anthem.

Also on Jamaican Tuff Gong 7", 'Songs Of Freedom', and a live version appears on 'Babylon By Bus'/'Rebel Music', segued into 'No More Trouble'.

RAT RACE
R MARLEY

Bob examines the arms race and finds it a rat race. Mentioning collective security on the road to sudden destruction, you get the feeling that here is a great song (credit: Rita) dashed off without being fully worked through. However, its impact has lasted. The vocal performance has a languor that sometimes jumps into what sounds almost like desperation.

Also on 'Rebel Music' and 'Songs Of Freedom'.

BOB MARLEY AND THE WAILERS

AFRICAN HERBSMAN

BOB MARLEY & THE WAILERS

Exodus

BOB MARLEY & THE WAILERS: 'EXODUS'

ISLAND ILPS 9498 3.6.77; REISSUES: MANGO ILPM 9498 30.3.87; CD CID 9498 19.1.87; TUFF GONG: TGLLP/CD 6 26.11.90

Changes were afoot between the recording of 'Rastaman Vibration' and 'Exodus'. After long tours to support 'Rastaman Vibration', The Wailers returned to Kingston in the Autumn of 1976 to find Jamaica in a state of emergency, as the country often was with an election upcoming (December 16). 'Rastaman Vibration' had sold better in America than its predecessors, and consequently its promotion had left the band drained. Chances are that its follow-up would be a tired, downbeat LP, even more so than 'Rastaman Vibration' itself, but fate was to intervene.

On December 3 two armed intruders burst into Bob's house at 56 Hope Road, Kingston, and opened fire. Don Taylor, Bob's manager, was hit five times. Two slugs missed, and one grazed Bob's chest and lodged in his arm. Rita Marley, in the yard, also took a bullet that scraped her skull. After playing at the Smile Jamaica Festival two days later, for which The Wailers had been booked for months, Bob left the country to convalesce in America, and then, in February 1977, he began to work on a new album in London.

The album was 'Exodus', and it was his most complete late work. The title was self explanatory, and Bob mentally extended his exile into an Old Testament tale of black repatriation. The sense of going-through-the-motions that some had detected in 'Rastaman Vibration' was gone, replaced by a dignity and intensity that drove the music forward. The title track itself seemed to be a new complicated synthesis of reggae and funk drawing considerable play on black US radio. There was the lighter side too, with 'Three Little Birds', 'Jamming' 'Waiting In Vain', and, eventually, 'One Love', all proving massive hits. Bob was back on track artistically and commercially, and the assassination attempt may have played a crucial role in his renaissance.

Marley had again been working with Lee Perry on several projects, and his influence is clear at several points in the LP. Above all else, maybe the scrape with death had led him to the conclusion that there was only so much time available to get his message across, and that message comes across far more clearly on 'Exodus' than on any other album. As 'Roots, Rock, Reggae' on the previous LP made clear, cracking the US market was uppermost in Bob's mind. The way that 'Exodus' was sequenced, with one song fading into the next in a couple of places, and with a thoughtful balance between message and love/party songs, suggests that someone at Island, or Bob himself, had given much thought to how the US could be seduced. The title, as well as its biblical connotation, also reflects Bob's town situation at the time: Jamaica was just too dangerous a place for him to be.

Perhaps responding to public demand, Canadian band Chalawa made a dub version of the LP, 'Exodus Dub', with their own rhythm tracks. Although 'Exodus'' musical structures are not that dissimilar to those of 'Rastaman Vibration', here we're getting the whole story, with the mixes acquiring a depth that the previous LP had failed to deliver. And, of course, Bob sounds inspired, a factor that would ignite any album.

Recorded: Harry J, Kingston, and Island Studios, London. Musicians: Marley, Aston & Carlton Barrett, Tyrone Downie, Earl 'Wire' Lindo, Alvin 'Seeco' Patterson, The I Threes; Junior Marvin (gtr); David Madden, Vin Gordon, Glen Da Costa, Dick Cuthell (horns).

Perhaps also: Phil Ramacon, Ibo Cooper (kbds); Angus Gaye (drums); Cat Coore (guitar).

Produced by: Bob Marley & The Wailers. All songs by Bob Marley unless stated.

NATURAL MYSTIC

Fading in, 'Natural Mystic' has a mesmeric intensity. Simple, musically repetitive, yet as powerful as anything Bob had cut for Island, it is the sound of smoke rising from the hills from a Rasta camp in Jamaica, even if it was cut in London.

This cut of the song is also on 'Songs Of Freedom'. In fact, this is not the only version of the song that Bob cut at the time. It was rumoured that Bob had made an entire LP at Lee Perry's Black Ark studios, and tracks have gradually emerged over the years. 'Natural Mystic' was one, and the alternative version, as gutsy, but perhaps lacking the uncomplicated intensity of this cut, finally showed up on 12" single (Daddy Kool Records UK) in 1986. It has also been sporadically available on various cheapo

European compilations along with 'Rainbow Country' (see 'The Upsetter Record Shop – Part 2') and older Perry-produced Marley material.

SO MUCH THINGS TO SAY

Milder, mellower than 'Natural Mystic', with Bob's lead vocal supported by The I-Threes, Bob rails against the "Spiritual wickedness in high places". Interestingly, the intense, freestyle of the lead vocal, with words running up against each other on certain lines, resembles the work of both Culture and Burning Spear, both of whom were at a peak of popularity in reggae at the time of this album's recording. The song climaxes in one such apparent improvisation, before a drum fill leads us into what we think, at first, is a dub mix, but instead turns out to be...

GUILTINESS

Perry's influence, in the flanged rhythm guitars and the tight, stacatto horn lines, perhaps informs 'Guiltiness'. Marley sounds supremely confident by now: no-one in the world could offer an opening triumvirate of songs like this. It's natural that 'Guiltiness' should follow 'So Much Things To Say', since its topic is similar: the unavoidable guilt and inevitable retribution that

must come to the "Big fish who always try to eat down the small fish".

THE HEATHEN

The intro and opening chorus of 'The Heathen' clearly betray Bob's apparent admiration for Burning Spear, and might, minus the pyrotechnical guitar solo from Junior Marvin, have come from Spear's 'Social Living' LP. There is, however, an intensity that is all Bob's, despite a light, beaten tone on the verses. That tone is apparently deliberate, as he calls for the embattled, poverty-stricken soldiers of blackness to rise again and drive back the heathen. With an air of dry menace in the chanted chorus, it's the perfect precursor for the title track.

EXODUS

Bob's most direct statement of Rasta repatriation doctrine. "Open your eyes, look within. Are you satisfied with the life you're living?" he sings. "We know where we're going, we know where we're from." Which is one and the same thing through Bob's eyes. The music has a powerful funk undertone. Another likely influence is Lee Perry, although rumours that Perry mixed the track are not really borne out by the sound. The song began as a studio jam, and at seven minutes 38 seconds, it's an epic, and virtually unique in reggae, although repatriation songs are common enough. No-one has made such a statement sound so biblical, however, and you can almost hear the marching of the Twelve Tribes of Israel in the rhythm.

It also appeared on UK & US 7" and 12" singles (WIP 6390, IXP-7; US IS 089) and Jamaican 7". All hold an instrumental cut on the flip except IS 089. The 12" mix of the song turns up on 'Songs Of Freedom'.

JAMMING

After the climax that was 'Exodus' itself comes the chill-out. Bob rediscovers the joy of partying, comparing it to a jam in the musical sense much as American funk musicians did, adding a sexual connotation, and the joy of unity between peoples. A massive hit, and a big influence on Stevie Wonder's 'Masterblaster' to boot. In case this seems to be Bob avoiding the depths of his abilities and the nightmare scenario of his shooting, take note of the line "No bullet can stop us now"; defiance while death was staring him in the eyes – not for the last time. Lovely fade out too, with a delicious rambling organ part quietly clos-

ing the track. The song was the one that Bob was playing when he called rival Jamaican political leaders, Michael Manley & Edward Seaga, up on stage at the One Love Peace Concert on April 22, 1988, in the hope of quelling violence between the parties' rival supporters.

Also on 7 & 12" singles (UK WIP 6410, US IS 092). The 12" mix is on 'Songs Of Freedom'.

WAITING IN VAIN

Immediately 'Jamming' closes, the count-in for 'Waiting In Vain', another classic, opens. Marley, with a tenderness he hadn't mustered since 'No Woman, No Cry', returns to the subject of 'I'm Still Waiting' (from 'The Best Of Bob Marley & The Wailers'), with similar chord structure but a thoroughly different approach. If Marley was forced to abandon reggae to make it as a US soul singer, here's the proof that he could have done it with style to spare, with an ease and carefree craft that was fast evaporating from the American brand with the dominance of disco.

A huge European hit in 1977 (UK WIP 6402, US IS 092) 'Waiting In Vain' is a largely under-rated song today. The 'previously promo-only 'Advert Mix' appears on 'Songs Of Freedom'.

TURN YOUR LIGHTS DOWN LOW

Taking the tempo down to an even milder level, here's a ballad, with bluesy guitar and Bob rambling his way through a song that seeks a fresh start from a lover that Bob knows he's neglected. Given stronger lyrics and a tighter reggae structure, this might have been another 'Waiting In Vain', but with a clutch of hits on 'Exodus' already, no-one was too worried about letting this, the slightest track on the album, slip by.

THREE LITTLE BIRDS

Another hit, although not until 1980 (WIP 6641), as heard on TV advertising throughout the Eighties, and one of Bob's mildest performances. The string sythesiser sound has dated badly and the message could be seen as trite in the light of what had been going on in Bob's life, but there's an innocence and delight in being alive in 'Three Little Birds'. Bob wrote it on the back step of his house at 56 Hope Road, and the three little birds were there collecting herb seeds discarded from spliffs that Bob rolled. The lyrics were supposedly addressed to Cindy Breakspeare, Jamaican beauty queen, one-time Miss World and Bob's lover.

Also available in an alternate mix on 'Songs Of Freedom'.

ONE LOVE/PEOPLE GET READY

Bob returns to an old Studio One hit (from 'The Wailing Wailers'), here given a slow, spiritual edge that's the opposite of the ska blast of the original. The interesting point is the mention of 'People Get Ready', the Curtis Mayfield song, in the title, and a Marley/Mayfield authorship credit to match. This is something of an unlikely owning-up, particularly when Mayfields' 'Keep On Moving' has always been credited to Marley.

It became a single in 1984 (US: 12IS(X) 169).

BOB MARLEY & THE WAILERS: 'KAYA'

ISLAND ILPS 9517 23.3.78; REISSUES: MANGO ILPM/CID 9517 30.3.87;
TUFF GONG TGLLP/CD 7 26.11.90

After the triumph of 'Exodus', Bob went out on the inevitable world tour, at first ignoring a football injury to a toe that had recurred from years before. Gradually, on tour, Bob's health began to wane, and by the time he took the limping foot to a specialist, amputation of the toe was recommended. Eventually another surgeon provided a skin-graft which appeared to solve the problem. With all this going on, there could be little time to put together another album to match 'Exodus', and no wonder 'Kaya' came nowhere near to equalling its predecessor's remarkable artistic flowering. Or so you would think: in fact, nearly all of the album emanated from the same sessions that produced 'Exodus'.

The title song, 'Sun Is Shining' and 'Satisfy My Soul' were all remakes, and the majority of the other material shied away from the intensity of the first half of 'Exodus', instead preferring what was, for the most part, love lyrics or what were apparently half-realised verses used over and over. Whether Bob was spreading himself too thinly at the time is a moot point, and perhaps he just wanted to put out an album with a different mood. Many of these songs – 'Running Away', 'Crisis', 'Time Will Tell' – might have been conceived as acoustic dope-fuelled jams (hence the return of 'Kaya'?) like Rasta 'Grounations'. Perhaps Bob wanted to put that unique atmosphere in a new context.

Although it received what might be described as mixed reviews at the time, it was still a far better album than 'Rastaman Vibration', and some of the performances rank with Bob's best. There were lots of horns on the original multi-track versions: by the time the album had been mixed most of them had been removed.

Recording details and musicians largely as previous entry. All songs by Bob Marley.

EASY SKANKING

A mild-mannered opener, with Bob pulling on a spliff while he rambles smokily through a song that extols the virtues of chilling out. There's some nice sax from Glen Da Costa (not, as the sleeve says, Vin Gordon, who supplied trombone) and that's about the long and the short of it. Less than essential, but passable.

Also on 'Songs Of Freedom'.

KAYA

Basically a brasher version of the old song cut for Lee Perry around 1971 (on 'Soul Revolution'). Gone is the subtle stoned feel, although the whispered backing vocal is retained in places, and the wandering gait of the mix and arrangement is far closer to that of a drunk than a stoned dread. The buzzing, almost jokey synth parts dropping in and out encourage that impression. Bob's vocal is not altogether convincing here either, suggesting that this is more of a performance than a return to a beloved old friend. Still it brought the word "kaya" back into common parlance as a euphemism for dope.

Also on US single (IS 49156).

IS THIS LOVE

Curiously, the track-listing provided by the lyrics printed on the back sleeve has 'Sun Is Shining' as the next track, suggesting that someone had been partaking of too much kaya and wasn't worried about the mistake, one that still lingers in

modern pressings of the LP. In fact the spliff plant that burns on the back sleeve (drawn by Paul 'Groucho' Smykle, better-known as a studio engineer) was a last-minute replacement for artwork deemed inappropriate for the album's title, reputedly a large portrait of Emperor Haile Selassie. The chief hit of the LP, 'Is This Love' is not the best-remembered Marley hit of today but was almost ubiquitous at the time. The song has an inexorable logic to it, circling from one part to the next with almost every line providing a hook drilled into your mind by the I-Threes. A carefree, glorious song, despite a rather odd reverb-filled mix and a bunch of little licks linking sections of the song that the band don't sound entirely comfortable with. A classic nonetheless.

Single: (WIP 6420 UK; IS 099). The full horns mix is available on 'Songs Of Freedom'.

SUN IS SHINING

Marley again tips his locks towards the past, with another song from the Lee Perry era ('Soul Revolution' LP). This version drops Peter Tosh's lonesome melodica, replacing it with Junior Marvin's hollowed-out lead guitar, although Tyrone Downie's organ is similar to some of Glen Adams' original. The mix aims at dub, but adds a rock element in the chunky guitars, making this version sound like a punk band's reggae impersonation with a brilliant rhythm section. The cold, lonesome atmosphere of the original is still here, and the song is still as baffling as ever: is Bob talking about love, and if the sun is so warming, why the grim melody? One of the great enigmas of Bob's songwriting career.

SATISFY MY SOUL

Another oldie, AKA 'Don't Rock The Boat', 'Rock My Boat' etc. (on 'Soul Revolution'). This version has a light, casual edge, as if Bob was making it up as he was going along. Once again The I-Threes are strongly in evidence, and the mixing again verges on dub. Not quite the equal of 'Is This Love', but Bob is so clearly the master of his musical destiny here that it seems churlish to criticise. This time, the bigger arrangement really adds something to the spartan original. Single (WIP 6440 UK).

For some strange reason, maybe to give you a jolt if you're falling into a stoned reverie under kaya power, after the song has finished and side one of the LP (the vinyl version at least) has come to a close, there's a clashing, honking sound like a car horn played backwards. It's curiously disturbing, as if everything is OK on the surface while a horrible reality is working away underneath. Or is that just because all was not well with Bob at the time, and we now know it, even if we weren't aware then? Perhaps it's just there as a technical error, like the awry track-listing, because that's how it turned out and if that's how it is, then that's how it is.

SHE'S GONE

Having been given a jolt, you'd expect a serious attack for the second half of the album, but it's not there, with Bob instead preferring a brief love song along 'Three Little Birds' lines without veering towards triteness. 'She's Gone' is similar to the sort of loose-limbed, cheery romantic skanks that Bob was concocting with Johnny Nash (the 'Chances Are' LP) or Leslie Kong ('Best Of The Wailers') at the tail-end of the Sixties. Perhaps if a little more work had been put into it, this might have been another hit.

MISTY MORNING

Bearing a similarly natural feel to 'She's Gone', but with a thicker, chunkier rhythm, replete with steaming horns from Zap Pow members Vin Gordon, Glen Da Costa and David Madden,

'Misty Morning' gets where it's going to in as much time as it takes, and won't be hurried. Bob, through a mix that's suitably foggy, offers just one verse, repeated twice, and a chorus to match. Exactly what he's on about is a mystery: maybe it's just about not feeling certain about your direction. 'Misty Morning' works because of the ease with which Bob's mastery of his genre makes something out of nothing, or maybe because it doesn't outstay its welcome.

CRISIS

The most solid skank of the album, and arguably one of the band's finest moments. Bob wants to give Jah the praises no matter what's going on in earthly realms. His vocal performance, all stuttery and dry, set in a distancing swathe of reverb, is decidedly peculiar, most resembling the sort of singing that Gregory Isaacs adopted in the mid-Eighties. The real star here is the loping rhythm, and you'll find that in all its glory on the instrumental version available on the flip of 'Is This Love' (WIP 6420 UK, IS 099 US, 1978).

RUNNING AWAY

Another remarkable Barrett Brothers' one-drop makes a lot from very little. 'Running Away', like 'Sun Is Shining', comes over like some strange improvisation, with Bob chanting a mantra of "You running and you running and you running away", repeatedly. Again the vocal performance is bizarre, dropping into a wheezy, peculiar old-codger sound for the last verse. Perhaps Bob was just trying a guide vocal and liked it. As for the song's provenance, the theme of futile escape has long been a favourite subject in reggae. Bob also throws in a smattering of 'Who Feels It Knows It' (from 'The Best Of Bob Marley & The Wailers') for good measure. Odd, hardly a song at all in the accepted sense, but strangely addictive. Also on 'Songs Of Freedom'.

TIME WILL TELL

Back to 'Burnin'' in style for a folky chant to close the album. The fundae, kette and repeater drums thunder, acoustic guitars strum and twang, and Bob offers a couple of lines over and over again, centred around *"Think you're in heaven but you're living in hell"*. The song was reputedly written as a kind of rebuttal of those who set him up to be shot. The last line of the sleeve's lyric-sheet says: "To be continued...", and the theme was, in that it provided the title for a 1992 Marley biographical movie.

BOB MARLEY & THE WAILERS: 'BABYLON BY BUS'
ISLAND ISLD 11 DOUBLE ALBUM, 1.9.78. REISSUES: TUFF GONG TGDLP/CD 1 26.11.90

The arrival of 'Babylon By Bus' marked a distinct change in press attitudes towards Marley. If 'Kaya' received mixed reviews, 'Babylon By Bus' drew a dismal response. It was released at a crucial time in Marley's career: he had established himself as one of the biggest live draws in the world, although America had not yet altogether succumbed to his charms in the record stores. There was sense in the media that Bob's roadshow had become something of a monster, that his outfit was another touring machine much like any other rock band: tonight, Deep Purple, tomorrow night, The Eagles, the day after, Bob Marley. With 'Kaya' selling well but seeming short on strong, worked-out material – new material anyway – and with a live album in the racks in the same year, some had suspicions that Bob had 'dried'. After all, wasn't a live album a way of keeping the punters happy while there was nothing else in the offing? Particularly one released a mere three years after the last one.

With a title drawn from a headline to a Penny Reel live review article in British music paper *NME* , 'Babylon By Bus' has come to represent something of a nadir in Marley's career for some observers. Chiefly recorded at the Paris Pavilion in June 1988 during a sprawling world tour, the whole approach of 'Babylon By Bus' could not be any more different from that of its 'Live!' predecessor. Whereas 'Live!' was a single album, evidently edited to keep the programme snappy, 'Babylon By Bus' offered two albums of the

Marley live experience in all its pomp and circumstance. While 'Live!' had hardly an announcement to punctuate the music, in direct opposition to most roots reggae gigs, which invariably featured the chant of "Jah Ras Tafari!", 'Babylon By Bus' spared no-one the opportunity to join in the exhortations. The chief critical arguments against the album today must be that none of the versions here are superior to the studio or other live cuts, that the songs were hurried, and, most telling of all for a Marley record, lack passion. The stretched songs probably worked fine in the mayhem of the live gigs, but here they just sound ready to snap. As for the crowd noise, it's too intrusive to let the music speak for itself, yet too anonymous to add excitement. There's none of the electricity, the sense of occasion, of the 'Live!' album.

However, Bob's Jamaican career continued as if unconnected with his worldwide role. His appearance at the One Love Peace Concert on April 22 1978 remains reggae's high-water mark when it comes to its ability to influence politicians. For once, the politicians weren't using reggae as a means to sell themselves, as they had done many times before: this time a reggae artist – Marley – forced the politicians to link hands with him onstage. It was an enforced unity before 30,000 people designed to stop the fighting between rival political gangs in Jamaica. Compared to this, the bleatings of the rock press were totally irrelevant.

The question remains as to why Island decided to put out another Marley in-concert set. At the time, rumours were rife that Marley was being courted by other labels; CBS and Atlantic were often mentioned. But since Bob never had a contract other than a handshake with Chris Blackwell, Island's boss, it can't have been a contractual fulfilment album knocked off just to keep what might have been the old record company happy. Anyway, the rumours never became more than just rumours. The truth is, 'Live!' was a huge success with the rock audience and 'Babylon By Bus', it was felt, might open up an even bigger one, in America particularly.

Production credits: Bob Marley & The Wailers.

Musicians: Marley, Astone & Carlton Barrett, Alvin 'Seeco' Paterson, Junior Marvin, Al Anderson, Earl 'Wire' Lindo, Tyrone Downie, The I-Threes.

Actual set list for the Paris night: 'Positive Vibration', 'Burnin' And Lootin'', 'Them Belly Full (But We Hungry)', 'Three O'Clock Road Block', 'War', 'No More Trouble', 'Running Away', 'Crazy Baldheads', 'Kinky Reggae', 'I Shot The Sheriff', 'No Woman No Cry', 'Is This Love', 'Jamming', 'Punky Reggae Party', 'Get Up, Stand Up', 'Exodus'.

Since other tracks not on the above set-list are included on the LP, perhaps they are drawn from the other dates suggested on the sleeve, in London, Copenhagen and Amsterdam. Also in the live set during the tour: 'Easy Skanking'.

POSITIVE VIBRATION

From 'Rastaman Vibration'. Bob gives a more assertive performance than the studio version, although the song is still short of Bob's finest. A strange choice for the opening of an album in the first place, never mind doing it twice.

PUNKY REGGAE PARTY

The only time 'Punky Reggae Party' has appeared on LP. Although the song, co-authored by Lee Perry, was popular amongst Bob's white fans in Europe at the time because of its lyrical attempt to marry punk and skank, this isn't the first song that you'd put on a list of Marley live classics. As a punk record, it's no more credible than most punk versions of reggae, and as a reggae record, it's little better than all the reggae records with 'skinhead' in their title at the turn of the Sixties. And either Carlie Barrett makes a rare error before the first verse, or there's a dodgy edit here.

EXODUS

From 'Exodus'. A live track that fades in? Apparently so, presumably executed at the editing stage. This excitable version takes the song at a slightly unseemly tempo, and the sound somehow doesn't hang together as it does on the original. The funk-style breakdown towards the end seems unnecessary. Bob's vocal sounds like a performance rather than the apparently natural singing of his best material.

Also appeared on promo single IPR 2026.

STIR IT UP

From 'Catch A Fire'. Having virtually rocked out on the first side, the second quarter of the LP starts out with a more sedate rocksteady tempo, even if it too is slightly hurried compared to the studio versions.

Appeared on UK 45 (WIP 6478, 1979).

RAT RACE

From 'Rastaman Vibration'. At last, a song that doesn't sound like it was desperate to be over. Marley gets serious, even if his voice is faintly flat at first.

Appeared on UK 45 (WIP 6478, 1979).

CONCRETE JUNGLE

From 'Catch A Fire'. Stretched to nearly six minutes, with a complex instrumental intro, the band puts down a steady, laid-back skank given a hard edge by the minor key. Bob's voice sounds

stretched and The I-Threes' parts don't seem to work properly, but the band are just great.

KINKY REGGAE

From 'Catch A Fire'. The 'missing' live track from the first 'Live!' album, given single release behind 'No Woman No Cry', makes it to album. Predictably, its casual, laconic skank and sexy lyric makes it one of Bob's best performances here: nothing seems strained. There's an even more relaxed live cut on 'Talkin' Blues'.

LIVELY UP YOURSELF

From 'Natty Dread'/'African Herbsman'. After a side of songs that were not anthems to a rock audience, Bob drops a real stirrer, adding a change in rhythm, and marginally, tempo, towards the end.

REBEL MUSIC

From 'Natty Dread'. Another anthem. Bob starts his part as if, melodically, he was already halfway through it. A passable version.

WAR/NO MORE TROUBLE

From 'Rastaman Vibration' and 'Catch A Fire'. Dynamite live on occasion, this version of 'War' is not the intense experience it should have been. Bob sounds committed enough, but somehow nothing else does. The segue into 'No More Trouble' makes logical sense.

Also appeared on a promo single (IPR 2026) and on 'Rebel Music'.

IS THIS LOVE

From 'Kaya'. A seven and a half minute version of a fine song really seems to be stretching the point, particularly the long intro.

HEATHEN

From 'Exodus'. Just when you're expecting hits all the way, Bob throws in the best roots performance of the entire album. Spoiled to an extent, unfortunately, by some distorted guitar soloing from Junior Marvin.

JAMMING

From 'Exodus'. An anthem. Bob was maybe bored with it by now, but he offers no indication of it. And here's the real drum and bass dub the album's been crying out for: you're left wanting more, a desire the rest of the album doesn't provoke. Left to the end of two slices of vinyl, that's far too late.

BOB MARLEY & THE WAILERS: 'SURVIVAL'

ISLAND ILPS 9542 2.10.'79; REISSUES: MANGO ILPM/CID 9542 30.3.87; TUFF GONG TGLLP/CD 8 26.11.90

Reputedly the first part of a planned three-album suite, together with the next two albums, 'Survival' was the first album cut at Bob's Tuff Gong studio. Originally titled 'Black Survival', it finds Bob more or less abandoning the lovers' lyrics and rambling 'talking blues' style of 'Kaya' and getting serious again. The sound is subdued, making the album sound more Jamaican and less 'produced' than most of its predecessors. The back of the sleeve, although slightly more organised than most Jamaican album sleeves with more than one photograph, and designed by the same designer Marley always favoured, Neville Garrick, somehow looks more 'reggae' than his other Island sleeves.

Bob was confronting his own demons as well as the world's: 'Ambush In The Night' tackled the assassination attempt on his life; 'Zimbabwe' was an ode to the emergent nation casting off the yoke of white Rhodesia; 'Wake Up And Live' exhorted those who accepted a life of poverty to rise. Bob was already ill with the cancer that killed him although no-one knew, not even the singer himself. However, he had thrown himself into his work because he felt he had a limited amount of time in which to influence events more serious than music, and also, maybe, because it was the best answer to worrying about things that would ultimately prove beyond his, or any-one's, control. The album is, incidentally, current-ly the most popular Marley LP in the UK reggae market at the time of writing (Autumn 1993), thanks to the presence of 'One Drop'.

Produced by Bob Marley & The Wailers & Alex Sadkin. Recorded at Tuff Gong.

Musicians: Marley, Aston & Carlton Barrett, Tyrone Downie, Earl 'Wire' Lindo, Junior Marvin, Al Anderson, Alvin 'Seeco' Patterson, The I-Threes, David Madden, Glen Da Costa, Vin Gordon; Anthony 'Sangie' Davis, Errol Brown, Aston Barrett (guitars); Headley Bennett (sax); Val Douglas (bass); Mikey 'Boo' Richards (drums).

All songs composed by Bob Marley & The Wailers unless otherwise noted in brackets.

SO MUCH TROUBLE IN THE WORLD

Musically, 'So Much Trouble In The World' is, in some respects, a throwback to the 'Soul Rebels' era. The swirling guitar chops meld into one, and the busy bass runs are also reminiscent of that era. But the middle-eight, a genuine Jamaican funky bridge, recalls the era when Marley was influenced by James Brown and The Temptations – particularly the ninth chords played by Al Anderson. Marley's vocal is comfortable, subdued, offering nothing of a performance as such, preferring sincerity – another factor that indicates a return to an era before commercial pressures closed in.

The "Million miles from reality," line also echoes The Temptations, being drawn from their 'Cloud Nine', a song which Marley was no stranger to (see 'Rebel's Hop' on 'Soul Rebels'). Here, however, he's not talking about drugs *per se*, but the way that a man can be sent into space – an ego trip, according to Marley – but can't get things right on earth. It's a similar theme to several US R&B records, notably Clay Tyson's 'Man On The Moon', Gil Scott-Heron's 'Whitey's On The Moon' and Howlin' Wolf's 'Coon On The Moon'. But instead of it being the central theme, Bob uses it as a small part of a broader message.

Also on UK 45 (WIP 6501) and 'Songs Of Freedom'.

ZIMBABWE

Soon to play the Zimbabwe independence ceremony, major recognition of Bob's status as the lone third world musician to become a superstar world-wide, the Gong here shakes out his locks in support of the apparently imminent retaking of Africa by black freedom fighters. While it's not a major Marley work, it was appropriate for its time and has a place in the history of political pop – particularly now that many black American musicians (Ice Cube and NWA in particular) have chosen to fight their battles on the home front first rather than choosing internationalism.

Also on UK single (WIP 6597, 7 & 12"), and 'Songs Of Freedom'.

TOP RANKIN'

Using a Seventies reggae catchphrase, Bob draws attention to a divide and conquer mentality in Jamaican politics, and like 'Jammin'', implies that you can't be into reggae and be divided. The wah-wah guitars prevalent in reggae at the time are very to the fore here, as are Carlie's rimshots and a thin, arid horn section.

BABYLON SYSTEM

Another chanty, Rasta song, although this time Bob concentrates more on the structure than he did on 'Kaya''s offering, 'Time Will Tell'. The acoustic piano here sounds incredibly similar to that on Bob's rocksteady era productions. The folksy, almost gospellish atmosphere is a throwback too, making it clear that Marley never forgot his time as a kid with a song in his head while another youth – Tosh – strummed a guitar in the yard. The lyric casts Babylon as a vampire, sucking the blood of the sufferers. "Tell the children the truth," urges Nosferatu-hunting Bob.

SURVIVAL

"We're the survivors, the black survivors," says Bob on a militant rhythm that resembles that of 'Exodus'. The lines about choosing the right way to live, and quickly, because time is running out, perhaps indicate that Bob feels that *his* time is draining away. (Whether this is because it was,

and he realised it, or whether it was because he felt that being involved in black politics even in the most general terms was likely to result in someone else taking a pot-shot at him is impossible to tell.) Not the match of 'Exodus', but a worthy addition to it.

Also on single (WIP 6553, 6597 UK; IS 49080 US), and 'Songs Of Freedom'.

AFRICA UNITE
MARLEY

Exactly what the title suggests: unification of black people and Africa, put in the inevitable Rasta context. The music, barring a flute lick (perhaps played on a synth), is very plain and simple indeed.

Also on 'Songs Of Freedom'.

ONE DROP
MARLEY

Reggae and unity with a big hoarse chorus, as in 'Jammin'', 'Trenchtown Rock', 'Lively Up Yourself' and many more. Lyrically, also a tribute to Carlie Barrett's drumming, in that he was the master of the 'one drop' drum pattern. Lee Perry later claimed authorship and covered the song.

Also on single (WIP 6610, 7 & 12" UK, IS 49156 US), and Jamaican Tuff Gong single with a dub version, both of which appear on 'Songs Of Freedom'.

RIDE NATTY RIDE
MARLEY

Rasta on a mission, with blueswailing harmonica (presumably from Lee Jaffe) and excellent lonesome trombone (from Vin Gordon). The song seems to ramble from section to section, throwing in some lyrics from 'Cornerstone' (from 'Soul Rebels') and promising apocalyptic fire. The I-Threes are in particularly fine form here, sounding the match of Aretha's Sweet Inspirations at one point. Shame they don't have something else to do other than simply echo Bob.

Also appears on 'Rebel Music'. The 12" mix (from UK single WIP 6610) is on 'Songs Of Freedom'.

AMBUSH IN THE NIGHT
MARLEY

Referring directly to his own encounter with a gunman, Bob attacks those who keep the people ignorant and therefore malleable enough to shoot at each other in the name of political parties. With a strong, heavy one drop and twanging clavinet in support, this is probably the best song on the album. Also appears as 'Ambush' on Tuff Gong 7" with a dub mix on the B-side.

WAKE UP AND LIVE
MARLEY/ANTHONY DAVIS

Another sub-'Exodus' song, looping on one riff and with a skin-tight horn section offering some contrast. Somehow it doesn't come off, despite the strength of the message. Bob is urging the band forward funky-style, and the chanted backing vocals resemble James Brown in 'Funky president' mode. This gives rise to a sneaking suspicion that Bob wasn't only plundering his funk-ish past, but also aiming at America. Co-author Anthony Davis was a regular at Tuff Gong at the time, writing for teenage singer Nadine Sutherland, and former lead singer of JA vocal group The Gatherers. In the band for what began as a jam: Val Douglas (bass); Mikey 'Boo' Richards (drums); 'Deadly' Headley Bennett (sax); Aston Barrett and Sangie Davis play guitar.

Also appears on UK 12" (WIP 6597).

BOB MARLEY & THE WAILERS: 'UPRISING'
ISLAND ILPS 9596; REISSUES: CD CID 9596 2.3.87; TUFF GONG TGLLP/CD 9 26.11.90

Marley, now occasionally bearing what author Timothy White has called "A sadness and a dread magnetism", set to work on the second album of his planned trilogy, another almost entirely serious work. It was to be the last album he would live to see released.

As with all of his late albums, it's not all wonderful, even if its political and social intent is perhaps more focused than ever before. There are some songs here that stand as true classics, however: 'Bad Card', a wry look at those he sees as his enemies; 'Work', which demanded that a better life couldn't be achieved by desire alone; 'Could You Be Loved', the only love song on the album, although even it contains some 'reality'; and 'Redemption Song', the acoustic ballad that has, in many respects, served as Bob's memorial.

The album wasn't altogether straightforward in coming together. Island boss Chris Blackwell reputedly turned down the LP in its original state, and 'Redemption Song' and 'Could You Be Loved' were late arrivals. Blackwell was concerned that the album was maybe a bit dour, and a pragmatic Bob could see his point. There were also a few songs which didn't make the final cut, some of which would later turn up on 'Confrontation', and some of which remain unissued to this day. With the privilege of owning his own studio, Marley could work with more or less anyone he liked, and in addition to the usual band. Carlton 'Santa' Davis was involved in the drum tracks, and several other musicians also worked on the album uncredited. The album, as was much of 'Confrontation', was recorded in the same sessions that produced 'Survival', Bob's last burst of studio creativity.

When 'Uprising' was released, Marley went out on the usual promotional tour, but it would never be completed. Perhaps it's just the harsh, grainy tones of Adrian Boot's photograph on the rear sleeve, or perhaps it's just hindsight, but a look at Marley's face as he crouches down amongst the band seems to tell us everything we need to know about his state of health: the rest of the band look tired from work; Bob looks tired from life. His voice sounds marginally thinner than it did. It may not be altogether coincidental that the photograph is printed over what looks like a sunset. The fact that the music retains the strength that matches the painting of a muscled Bob rising from the earth at sunrise on the front sleeve shows Bob's sheer determination to rage against the dying of the light.

All songs by Bob Marley

COMING IN FROM THE COLD

"Why do you look so sad and forsaken, when one door is closed, don't you know another is open?" A hoarse, breathless Bob outlines the minimal importance of a single man compared to the breadth of life itself, without forgetting the importance of all people as equals. It could almost be a message of hope to those he would soon leave behind him. Bob wrote it while recovering from his foot injury – cancerous – in Miami. "The biggest man you ever did see was once a baby in this life," he sings, over a plain, no-frills skank. The lyric-sheet on the sleeve, incidentally, contains a spelling mistake which, perhaps out of respect for how it was when the singer was alive,

has gone uncorrected, if not unnoticed.

The song was also a Jamaican Tuff Gong single, with a dub mix on the flip. The 12" mix, from US single (IS 49636) is available on 'Songs Of Freedom'.

REAL SITUATION

Bob gets apocalyptical in a matter-of-fact way. The "Once a man, twice a child," in the song is a Jamaican proverb of Biblical extraction: Bunny Wailer once used it on an obscure single 'All Over' (1971). Another message to those who will outlive Bob turns up in the form of "Everything is just for a while", another folk saying that takes on a new resonance in the light of later events. Also on 'Songs Of Freedom'.

BAD CARD

One of the better-known late Marley works, 'Bad Card' is Bob predicting the inevitable crumbling of the structures of oppression – or simply those who try to thwart his daily business. The "I want to disturb my neighbour 'cause I'm feeling so right", is strangely reminiscent of the "Feel like bombing a church" line in 'Talkin' Blues' (from 'Natty Dread'), although here Bob is talking about joy in his own beliefs rather than his disgust with others' lies. With an acoustic piano providing a churchy skank, 'Bad Card' is a song that quietly grows on the listener. There's great footage of Bob rehearsing the song on the 'Caribbean Nights' video.

Also on 'Songs Of Freedom'.

WE AND THEM

Bob declares that he has no friends in high places. Perhaps not strictly true, but in a song that demands reparations for the blood of poor children and slaves, such points are mere pedantry. As with most of the first half of this album, the music is a plain, unfussy skank, although at one point a male vocal group offer a fair impression of what the original Wailers might have contributed to the song had they still been together.

WORK

It was becoming a habit to put the most solid, militantly-arranged song on the album at the end of side one, and 'Work' is no exception. A bluesy, looping, faintly funky examination of the endless work required in life, whether you're working for a living or working for the greater good. "If you ain't got nothing to do," says Bob, like a youth-club preacher confronted by surly, time-killing kids, "Work, we got some work for you." Considering that, it might be argued, the singer worked himself to death instead of getting treatment for whatever was ailing him, 'Work' is a brave declaration of a philosophy that couldn't abide the frittering away of Jah's time.

The 'Work' on Jamaican Tuff Gong 7" (1976) is an instrumental entirely unconnected with this song.

ZION TRAIN

Returning to his roots, Bob offers another variant along the lines of 'This Train'/'People Get Ready' (see 'One Love' LP). The song has been heard before, but the band's impeccable, rock- solid support makes this something else. Carlie Barrett's drumming has a force here that must be heard to be appreciated. The lyric sheet offers a few lines on the final chorus, a particularly Mayfieldesque few lines, that never appeared on the record owing to an early fade-out.

PIMPER'S PARADISE

Bob was rarely critical of women on record, so 'Pimper's Paradise', a soulish dismissal of a wayward female who fell into the sort of lifestyle that would make her the victim of a pimp, is almost unique. Even so, this is a long way short of a scathing attack, and Bob, at the end, is just as keen to blame the exploiters as the exploited. The attitude is, needless to say, an entire philosophy different from that of the rappers who celebrated pimping a decade later.

COULD YOU BE LOVED

'Could You Be Loved' gave 'Uprising' a hit single, littered in croaking clavinet and scratchy guitar. The tone is slightly shrill, which suggests that perhaps it was speeded up in tempo slightly while being mastered. If that seems unlikely or harsh, Island Records had done it before for Burning Spear's 'Marcus Garvey' LP, and it remains a little tinkering trick for record companies to this day; besides which, was it not better to obtain a song's full commercial potential and help sell the LP in order to disseminate Bob's message?

Although 'Could You Be Loved' sounds like a love song, it isn't: in fact, Bob is emphasising how important it is to be yourself – slightly ironic considering that the guitar licks had been 'borrowed' from a mildly famous funk record, and especially if the tempo had been raised for promotional purposes. However, it worked, and Bob's song was

a must in the hipper commercial discos, and it had a message that the songs it was played alongside couldn't offer. The song, needless to say, stands out like a sore thumb on the album.

Other versions: a 12" mix appears on 'Songs Of Freedom', originally from UK single (WIP 6610, later reissued on US 422-875 676-4). The song, incidentally, provoked a court dispute between Danny Sims, Marley's former publisher, and the singer's estate over ownership. It was later covered by Anglo-US pop band Shakespeare's Sister.

FOREVER LOVING JAH

Back to the slow skanks with an almost brutal opening to a song that echoes several in Bob's past: most recently, 'Crisis' (from 'Kaya'), in the deeper past, 'Rudie', with the line "What has been hidden from the wise and prudent has been revealed to the babes and sucklings", forming 'Ruddie''s fade-out (see 'Best Of The Wailers'). It's not the only folk-saying here, by any means: 'Forever Loving Jah' is like a dictionary of quotations. Written soon after the assassination attempt, it has a certain determination and strength, and is one of the highlights of the LP.

Also on 'Songs Of Freedom'.

REDEMPTION SONG

Although regarded by some as lyrically out of character, 'Redemption Song' is perhaps Marley distilled to his essence – the spiritual side of him, at least. As for the lone voice accompanied by his acoustic guitar, this really isn't so far removed from the chants and gospellish sing-alongs that pepper Bob's career – the rocksteady cut of 'This Train' (unavailable on album, unfortunately), 'Rasta Man Chant' ('Burnin''), 'Time Will Tell' (from 'Kaya') – among them. As for the message, casting aside fears of man's vain and warlike science for a belief in a greater power, no more eloquent appeal on behalf of any religious belief was ever constructed. As for the historical opening verse, it comes as particularly poignant considering Bob's own black and white parentage. And, perhaps, not only is Bob saying that his own songs are here to redeem, it seems like he's casting aside older songs of redemption too. That's why the line "Emancipate yourself from mental slavery", is central to Bob's way of life: even the religion he was taught as a child, the redemption songs that he declares were "All I ever had" were false, leading him in a direction that did not liberate him or his people.

As for the autobiographical element, casting himself as a singer and freedom fighter, this is not Bob as a *player* of reggae, as he was in 'Trenchtown Rock' and 'Lively Up Yourself', it is Bob as the music itself. It was all he ever had, it was all he was. As conceptually complex and yet musically simple as it was, 'Redemption Song' shows Bob as capable of looking at himself from several viewpoints at once, as well as offering hope and dignity for a future that he wouldn't personally share. It is little wonder that the song, never a chart hit, and added to the album at the last minute, became his epitaph.

Also on single (WIP 6653, with a band version on flip, UK; IS49636 US). A version from Bob's last-ever performance appears on 'Songs Of Freedom'. Saxophonists Dean Fraser (1984) and Courtney Pine (1992) have covered it.

BOB MARLEY & THE WAILERS 'CONFRONTATION'
ISLAND ILPS 9760 23.5.83; REISSUES: MANGO ILPM/CID 9760 30.3.87; TUFF GONG TGLLP/CD 10 26.11.90)

The final part of Bob's trilogy emerged after his death. It almost certainly wasn't the same album he had envisaged, although the title and Neville Garrick's artwork, with Bob in a St George-style pose driving a spear into the heart of a dragon, were as conceived. The music is a hotch-potch of old-ish and new tracks, none of which had turned up on an album before. 'Chant Down Babylon' was an out-take from 'Uprising'; 'Buffalo Soldier', a posthumous European hit, had been originated by King Sporty (a long-time reggae DJ/singer, now based in Miami and married to soul diva Betty Wright: see 'Ska Jerk' on 'One Love); 'Blackman Redemption' and 'Rastaman Live Up!' were both one-off singles on Tuff Gong in 1978 although the latter is very different here; 'Trench Town' had been a posthumous Tuff Gong 45 in 1982; 'Stiff Necked Fools' was a song that had been kicking around in at least two versions for several years.

Inevitably it's a patchy album, but no more so than 'Uprising' or 'Survival', and arguably, it has a brightness and optimism that those two do not. Its connection to those albums is reinforced by the quote, "Dem a go tired fe see me face, Can't get me out a the race", that adorns the top of the by-now inevitable lyric sheet on the rear sleeve. The line comes from 'Bad Card', from Uprising', and says, clearly, that even in death his message will live on to chasten his enemies.

All songs written by Bob Marley unless noted.

CHANT DOWN BABYLON
An out-take from 'Uprising'. The theme of 'Chant Down Babylon' is a long-standing one in reggae and a tradition that goes back to Rasta grounations, when chanting to drums and any other instruments that were available while under the influence of meditation-inducing ganja was a bonding process, both within the community, with God, and with the earth. Marley's version is not a chant at all as such, compared to

'Rasta Man Chant' (from 'Burnin'') for example, but an upright one-drop that explains reggae as the messenger by which Bob knows that Babylon must be destroyed. The one-drop drumming here, incidentally, is not that of Carlie Barrett, but Carlton 'Santa' Davies, which probably explains why he got a thank you on 'Uprising'.

BUFFALO SOLDIER

Bob recalls the arrival of black people in America and their conscription into the army, using a term that Native Americans invented, and extends the epithet to Rastas. A brief history lesson, the bright, busy skank gave Bob a huge post-humous hit.

JUMP NYABINGI

Another song that had been kicking around unused for a long time, 'Jump Nyabingi' dates from around the release of 'Kaya', as the horn section, reverbed rimshots and then-fashionable Moog sounds indicate. The word 'Nyabingi' here indicates Rastaman, although originally it meant those originating from a certain African tribe, commonly called Nyahmen in Jamaica. The song basically celebrates Rasta unity through dancing.

MIX UP, MIX UP

Another older song, probably from the same era as 'Jump Nyabingi', or maybe even earlier. The vocal is idiosyncratic enough to suggest that Bob hadn't altogether finished with it, although it's probably too organised to just be a guide voice. Chances are the backing vocals, and possibly the string-synth, were added later.

GIVE THANKS & PRAISES

Probably a late track, circa 'Uprising', 'Give Thanks & Praises' is a prayer on vinyl, with Bob sounding so laid-back that it might be at the end of a long day spent spliffing up, and the band providing a steady, but equally easy-going skank behind him. Certainly one of the better tracks here, simply because it is so casually executed and peaceful. Thematically similar to the much earlier 'Thank The Lord' (on 'Songs Of Freedom'/'In The Beginning'), it was originally demoed in 1980, but not finished until 1983 for this album. Also on 'Songs Of Freedom'.

BLACKMAN REDEMPTION
BOB MARLEY/LEE PERRY

A single in 1978, 'Blackman Redemption' was co-authored and produced by Lee Perry, although few of his trademark production devices are here: what there are, the buzzing horn section and ticking production must be counted amongst their number. In fact a far more typical Perry mix exists, although it has never seen release except on sound-system dub-plate (acetate). Lyrically the song is a history lesson and an examination of Rasta doctrine.

TRENCH TOWN

Bob returns to Kingston 12, offering a more idyllic version of Rasta life there than many would imagine. As laid-back as the two preceding tracks, with tasteful guitar, warm, open-sounding horns and a hypnotic bassline, 'Trench Town' is perhaps the most pleasing, complete song on the album, and probably comes from the same sessions that delivered 'Survival'.

STIFF NECKED FOOLS

Bob attacks... who? The rich? The pompous? Those with starched, reversed collars? Whoever it is, Bob sounds very confident on the song, one that holds a small but important place in reggae history although you wouldn't know it from this version. Before cutting this incarnation of 'Stiff Necked Fools', Bob demoed the song with some

youths who were trying to make their way on the Kingston studio scene, Cleveland Browne (drums) and Wycliffe Johnson (keyboards). It was the first time they were to work together, but as Steely & Clevie they were to rule reggae as an electronic rhythm from the mid-Eighties onwards, much as The Barrett Brothers had done in the early Seventies. This version of the song is slow and minimal enough to make it a precursor of the sort of beat that would give rise to Steely & Clevie's dominance: dancehall.

I KNOW

More evidence that commercial pressures to make it in America had caused Bob to experiment with a few adjustments to his style, or simply a return to mid-Sixties R&B roots? After an intro that recalls 'I Shot The Sheriff', Bob shouts a ballad in praise of Jah at the top of his voice, probably recorded circa 1978. Certainly not properly worked out at the time of recording, 'I Know' sounds like it's in the wrong key for Bob, and was probably abandoned as a disaster at the time of recording. It's certainly the least Marleyesque track of his Island career, and arguably the worst. Intriguingly though, stripped down, a very similar beat to the one Bob was trying out here would also fuel the rise of Maxi Priest and Shabba Ranks, two reggae stars who did get to sell records in America big-time while still alive.

RASTAMAN LIVE UP
BOB MARLEY/LEE PERRY

A Tuff Gong single in 1978 produced by Lee Perry, this different, Perry-free cut of the song lacks the ease of the earlier version, although lyrically this edition is more developed. With a faintly brittle rhythm and strained singing, it seems likely that this is another out-take from 'Survival', as the keep-on-trying theme suggests. It was probably put aside at the time owing to the rough vocal: the rhythm track was remade for this LP in 1983.

Also on 'Songs Of Freedom'.

POSTHUMOUS COMPILATIONS

VARIOUS ARTISTS: 'COUNTRYMAN, THE ORIGINAL SOUNDTRACK FROM THE FILM'
ISLAND MSTDA 1, 1982

Includes the following Marley/Wailers tracks: 'Natural Mystic', 'Rastaman Chant', 'Rat Race', 'Jah Live', 'Three O'Clock Road Block', 'Small Axe', 'Time Will Tell', 'Pass It On'.

BOB MARLEY & THE WAILERS: 'THE BOX SET'
ISLAND BMSP 100, 1982

The following Marley/Wailers LPs in a set, in different sleeves, with lyrics. 10,000 copies only, aimed at the US, although copies turned up worldwide. Not to be confused with other Marley box sets such as 'Songs Of Freedom', etc: 'Catch A Fire'; 'Burnin''; 'Natty Dread'; 'Live!'; 'Rastaman Vibration'; 'Exodus'; 'Kaya'; 'Survival'; 'Uprising'.

THE WAILERS: 'REGGAE GREATS'
MANGO MLPS 9575, 1984, US ONLY

A compilation that formed part of Island's 'Greats' series of reggae reissues and probably helped to promote the first two, comparatively poorly-selling Wailers LPs for the label. Details as per 'Catch A Fire' and 'Burnin''. Tracks: 'Concrete Jungle', 'No More Trouble', 'Get Up Stand Up', 'Rock It Baby', 'Burnin' And Lootin'', 'Small Axe', 'Pass It On', 'Midnight Ravers', 'Stop That Train', 'Rastaman Chant'.

BOB MARLEY & THE WAILERS: 'LEGEND'
ISLAND BMW 1 8.5.84. PICTURE DISC PBMW 1 28.5.84. CD CID 103 27.8.85, TUFF GONG TGDCD 1 26.11.90

Bob's greatest hits, originally in their single mixes rather than album incarnations, with liner notes by Timothy White & Rob Partridge. An eternal seller, the sort of album that every artist and company wants on the catalogue. The original American version differed slightly in that it contained dance mixes by Eric Thorngren of 'No Woman, No Cry', 'Buffalo Soldier', 'Waiting In Vain', 'Exodus' and 'Jamming'. Chris Blackwell commissioned the mixes in the hope of scoring some belated dance-floor hits in America, but which met limited success. The American pressing has now reverted to the same format as the British one.

That's not the end of the story, however. Due to an oversight, when 'Legend' was digitally remastered, the album tapes were ordered up rather than the single versions. Therefore, tracks like 'Could You Be Loved' and 'No Woman No Cry' appear in a different form from those on the first pressing. Considering the sales figures for the LP, it's astonishing that they haven't plundered the back catalogue a little more. There is, however, a 'Legend 2' being planned for release sometime in 1994, although a track-listing is not yet available. Among likely candidates for anthologising are 'Iron Lion Zion', 'Nice Time' and 'Punky Reggae Party'.

Tracks: 'Is This Love', 'No Woman No Cry', 'Could You Be Loved', 'Three Little Birds', 'Buffalo Soldier', 'Get Up, Stand Up', 'Stir It Up', 'One Love/People Get Ready', 'I Shot The Sheriff', 'Waiting In Vain', 'Redemption Song', 'Satisfy My Soul', 'Exodus', 'Jamming'.

BOB MARLEY & THE WAILERS: 'REBEL MUSIC'
ISLAND ILPS 9843 16.6.86. TUFF GONG REISSUE TGGLP/CD 11 26.11.90

Bob's greatest hits for those with a rebellious bent. Not the seller that 'Legend' was, but a fine collection nonetheless. Sleevenote on UK and US pressings: Neil Spencer.

Tracks: 'Rebel Music (3 O'Clock Roadblock)' (Paul 'Groucho' Smykle remix), 'So Much Trouble In The World', 'Them Belly Full (But We Hungry)', 'Rat Race', 'War/No More Trouble' ('Babylon By Bus' version), 'Roots' (previously available only as the flip to 'Waiting In Vain' single), 'Slave Driver', 'Ride Natty Ride', 'Crazy Baldhead', 'Get Up, Stand Up'.

BOB MARLEY & THE WAILERS: 'TALKIN' BLUES'
TUFF GONG TGLLP 12, 4.2.91

A surprisingly low-key project, 'Talkin' Blues' combines in-concert performance with radio sessions and the occasional studio out-take to produce an unarguably excellent sidelong look at Marley's early Island career. The tracks are punctuated by ten snippets of a September 1975 interview between Bob and journalist Dermot Hussey. The majority of the material derives from a live-in-session event at the Record Plant, Sausalito, California, in October 1973, recorded for KSAN-FM, a San Francisco radio station.

The band line-up for the session was Bob (guitar/vocals), Peter Tosh (guitar/vocals), Earl 'Wire' Lindo (keyboards), Aston & Carlton Barrett (bass & drums), and Joe Higgs (vocals/percussion). Higgs replaced Bunny Wailer, who, although he had not officially left the band, disliked touring. Higgs had known The Wailers since their early days at Studio One, and was widely credited with being their mentor in the art of harmony vocals. Here are The Wailers at their most minimally elegant, Jamaican funky and apparently at home as they never sounded on the other official live releases.

The final track on the album, 'I Shot The Sheriff', is a version from the first night of the two London concerts that produced the 'Live!' LP. For musicians, see the entry for 'Live!'

The other three tracks were out-takes from the 'Natty Dread' sessions, one of which, 'Am A

Do', never saw release elsewhere. For musicians, see the entry for 'Natty Dread'.

The bright, informative sleevenotes for the album are by former *Melody Maker* journalist Rob Partridge, who worked for Island Records during Bob's peak years and is the UK PR for his catalogue today.

TALKIN' BLUES

A variant on the song to be found on 'Natty Dread'. Mildly slacker in tempo, and a shade drier in approach, it sounds even more casual than the version we're used to. There's no acoustic guitar, no harmonica, and The I-Threes' vocals are slightly less smooth and far more charming. Of most interest, however, is the final section, which is altogether different, lyrically, from the 'Natty Dread' cut, offering a Rastafarian resistance in the face of derision from the outside world.

BURNIN' AND LOOTIN'

Live session. Bob's voice is agreeably lonesome at the start. The skanky guitar and bristling clavinet are excellent. Harmonies are far rougher than on the studio cut.

KINKY REGGAE

Live session. A terrific version of one of the most under-rated Marley songs. Tosh's support vocals are marvellously crisp. The band sounds about as small as would be adequate here, with Wire's organ filling out the gaps.

GET UP, STAND UP

Live session. Tosh and Marley spar on a strong cut of their co-authored militant anthem.

SLAVE DRIVER

Live session. Reduced to basics, this version of 'Slave Driver' has a mysterious downbeat atmosphere a mile different from the version on 'Catch A Fire'.

WALK THE PROUD LAND

Live session. The absent Bunny Wailer's Studio One rude boy anthem given a laconic, easy, jamming treatment with Bob taking lead and Higgs and Tosh in strong support. Probably totally indecipherable to the radio audience, the "Ska quadrille" line is changed to "skank quadrille". Bunny would later have another crack at it on his 'Sings The Wailers' LP.

YOU CAN'T BLAME THE YOUTH

Live session. Tosh on a song not released by The Wailers for Island, although he later did it for his own Intel Diplo label (1974). Clearly a lamented absentee from The Wailers' catalogue, it finds Tosh defending youth rebellion on the grounds that the kids were told lies all the way through their upbringing. Wire's keyboards are excellent.

RASTAMAN CHANT

Live session. As casual as anything they ever recorded, The Wailers stroll gently through their grounation chant (AKA 'Rasta Man Chant'/'Chant I') from 'Burnin''.

AM A DO

'Natty Dread' out-take. A reduced skank identified as work-in-progress on the sleeve, 'Am-A-Do', with its "Do it with your bad self" chorus, is another examination of Bob's sexy lover's rock style combined with his apparent crush on US funk. Who knows what this might have become had it been finished – perhaps another 'Kinky Reggae'?

BEND DOWN LOW

'Natty Dread' out-take. The Wailers' mid-Sixties hit in an alternate version, without The I-Threes except as spill from an unused track, and littered in the flute that informed only part of the released version. The rhythm is altogether lighter-stepping than on 'Natty Dread', and the song suddenly stops without ever reaching the end, presumably because Bob wanted to change something.

I SHOT THE SHERIFF

Live at the Lyceum, London. Vocally a little more gentle than the released cut, although it sounds maybe a shade more sincere.

BOB MARLEY & THE WAILERS: 'SONGS OF FREEDOM'

TUFF GONG FOUR-CD SET TGCBX1, 21.9.92; ALSO AVAILABLE AS AN EIGHT-ALBUM VINYL SET IN JAMAICA, TGLBX1, 10.5.93

A serious collection from Island that sets out to offer material unavailable elsewhere, alternate mixes, obscure Jamaica-only releases, while attempting to detail Marley's career in all of its phases from first to last. It succeeds. Packaged in bookshelf format, with sleevenotes from Rita Marley, Rob Partridge, Timothy White, Chris Salewicz, Rabbit and Derrick Morgan, this is the compilation that all others must live up to. In a numbered limited edition of one million, with 750,000 sold worldwide at the time of writing! In case you were wondering, Bob's mother, Cedella Booker, got number one.

CD 1

JUDGE NOT

Bob's first single, a fast ska tune as close to his "be yourself" message as anything he ever recorded. Produced by Leslie Kong, Feb 1962. A UK Island/ Beverly's JA single as Robert Marley.

ONE CUP OF COFFEE

Bob's second single, released on Jamaican pressing as by Bob Martell. Rumour has it that a third Beverly's single, 'Terror', was pressed as Bob Martin. At least dogs would have liked it. Details as previous entry.

SIMMER DOWN Details: 'The Wailing Wailers' **I'M STILL WAITING** Details: 'The Wailing Wailers'. The shorter version. **ONE LOVE/PEOPLE GET READY** Details: 'The Wailing Wailers' **PUT IT ON** Details: 'The Wailing Wailers'. The mix with extra guitars, as on the 'One Love' album.

BUS DEM SHUT (PYAKA)

One of the most obscure, and best, of The Wailers' records for their first self-owned label, 'Wail'N Soul'M'. Not really a Jamaican hit, but the "Bah bah bah bah bah" vocal device proved popular enough to turn up in reggae years later on The Immortals' 'Why Keep A Good Man Down'. If food and drink is the stuff of life, asks Bob on a stately, mild rocksteady rhythm, then how come some of us have to "bus dem shut" to get it, meaning to work so hard that your shirt is ripped asunder.

MELLOW MOOD

The original cut, for 'Wail'N Soul'M, of this famous Marley song, also recorded by Johnny Nash. Once again this is the remarkably haughty rocksteady this early self-produced (1966-8) material is celebrated for.

BEND DOWN LOW Details: 'The Best Of Bob Marley & The Wailers' **HYPOCRITES** Details: 'All The Hits'

STIR IT UP

The original rocksteady cut, for Wail'N Soul'M, of the song later covered by Johnny Nash and remade by The Wailers for 'Catch A Fire'.

NICE TIME Details: 'All The Hits'. There's a brief count-in on this pressing.

THANK YOU LORD

The original, effortless rocksteady version produced for Wail'N Soul'M, 1967. Also on the 'All The Hits' album. Later versions appear on 'In The Beginning', 'The Early Years 1968-74', a Trojan single, and on a 1972 Tuff Gong 45.

HAMMER

Recorded in 1968 for JAD, this light, unprepossessing rocksteady performance, with a somewhat over-exposed chorus and unlikely harmonies from Bunny & Rita, is similar in sentiment to 'Small Axe', although far less celebrated. Rumour has it that this was a demo.

CAUTION Details: 'The Best Of The Wailers' **BACK OUT** Details: 'The Best Of The Wailers' **SOUL SHAKEDOWN PARTY** Details: 'The Best Of The Wailers' **DO IT TWICE** Details: 'The Best Of The Wailers' **SOUL REBEL** Details: 'Soul Rebels' **SUN IS SHINING** Details: 'Soul Revolution' **DON'T ROCK THE BOAT** Details: 'Soul Revolution' **SMALL AXE** Details: 'African Herbsman' **DUPPY CONQUEROR** Details: 'Soul Revolution' **MR BROWN** Details: 'Soul Revolution 1 & 2'

CD2

SCREW FACE Details: 'The Upsetter Record Shop Part II'

LICK SAMBA

From 1971, 'Lick Samba' is an ode to the joys of sexy girls. A Marley production, it was a JA Tuff Gong and UK Bullet (BU 493) single. The Wailers, bolstered by the presence of Rita, are in fine form here.

TRENCHTOWN ROCK Details: 'African Herbsman' LP. This is an alternate, and probably

superior, mix. "I'm groovin'," says Bob, "and the world know it by now." Soon enough they would.

CRAVEN CHOKE PUPPY

A steady, tight-strutting skank that uses the title in more than one way. Not only is the metaphor in effect – a craven dog, losing its bone for another it can't get – but also the strength of Craven A tobacco, popular in Jamaica at the time, too strong for a youth anxious to take over. A pop at those looking to take what isn't rightfully theirs. A rare Tuff Gong single from 1972, there's also a DJ version by Big Youth ('Craven Version', Tuff Gong, 1972).

GUAVA JELLY

One of Bob's early international songwriting successes, co-written with Bunny, covered by Johnny Nash and Barbra Streisand. A song full of 'island charm', innocent enough to outsiders but explicitly sexy to those in the know. A Tuff Gong/UK Green Door 45, 1971/2.

ACOUSTIC MEDLEY

Previously unreleased. Bob and guitar in Sweden, 1971, in the presence of Johnny Nash and John 'Rabbit' Bundrick with a rolling tape recorder. Not quite as unique a document as it seems: the Tuff Gong vaults hold several similar tapes, generally recorded at 56 Hope Road in the kitchen. Faintly, in the background, you can hear another voice, probably Nash's. The songs here: 'Guava Jelly', 'This Train', 'Cornerstone', 'Comma Comma', 'Dewdrops', 'Stir It Up', 'I'm Hurting Inside'. A soulful, personal performance.

I'M HURTING INSIDE

Bob and the unmistakable sound of British reggae in its anaemic, bowdlerised infancy. Cut in 1971 and produced by Johnny Nash in London, it's a song that The Wailers made such a beautiful rocksteady single with for their own Wail'N Soul'M label circa 1967. Here it's just a kitsch curio. This mix is different, incidentally, from that found on 'Chances Are'.

HIGH TIDE OR LOW TIDE

AKA 'High Seas Or Low Seas', and intended for release on 'Catch A Fire', this mild, hardly-mixed soulful performance sounds low-key enough to be a demo. There's an earlier cut of this somewhere in the vaults. A Tuff Gong production, circa 1972, and unreleased until this set.

SLAVE DRIVER Details: 'Catch A Fire'

NO MORE TROUBLE Details: 'Catch A Fire'
CONCRETE JUNGLE Details: 'Catch A Fire'
GET UP, STAND UP Details: 'Burnin''
RASTAMAN CHANT Details: 'Burnin''
BURNIN' & LOOTIN' Details: 'Burnin''

IRON LION ZION

Unreleased until now, later to be a huge European hit (1992) when comprehensively re-produced after Bob's death, this is the original raw version, a tough skank with bubbly guitar. The line "My brothers want to be the stars, so they fighting tribal wars", is a direct reference to the recently departed Bunny & Peter, and this is one of the first recordings, circa early 1974, that Bob made without their presence. From here on in, it was Bob and the I-Threes all the way.

LIVELY UP YOURSELF Details: 'Natty Dread' **NATTY DREAD** Details: 'Natty Dread' **I SHOT THE SHERIFF (LIVE)** Details: 'Live!'

NO WOMAN NO CRY (LIVE AT THE ROXY)

A different, previously unissued live version of the song from 'Natty Dread' and 'Live!'. Recorded at the Roxy, Los Angeles, 26 May,

1976. Even slower than the hit version, as if it was being taken to its logical, spiritual extreme.

WHO THE CAP FIT Details: 'Rastaman Vibration'

JAH LIVE

At last, the song that Bob cut with Lee Perry at Harry J Studio as a response to the announcement of HIM Haile Selassie's death in 1976, and released almost immediately after on Tuff Gong, and later Island, single, gets an album release. A slow, totally self-assured performance, it has a mellow, rock-solid confidence that outlined Bob's total faith in his chosen lifestyle perhaps more than any other record he cut.

CRAZY BALDHEADS Details: 'Rastaman Vibration' **WAR** Details: 'Rastaman Vibration' **JOHNNY WAS** Details: 'Rastaman Vibration' **RAT RACE** Details: 'Rastaman Vibration'

JAMMIN'

The 12" single mix, a longer, initially leaner, eventually epic version. Details: 'Exodus'

WAITING IN VAIN The 'Advert mix', originally on the flipside of the promo single. With a rough bit of toasting from Bob as an intro, and a chunkier, faintly dubbier mix. Details: 'Exodus' **EXODUS** 12" mix. A seven minute-plus cut with a ringing dub ending. Details: 'Exodus'. **NATURAL MYSTIC** Details: 'Exodus' **THREE LITTLE BIRDS** Previously unreleased alternate mix, a shade more echoing, with a mellow bluesy guitar part. Details: 'Exodus' **RUNNING AWAY** Details: 'Kaya'

KEEP ON MOVING

The 'London Version'. Produced by Lee Perry, with musicians that include Drummie of Aswad, Richie Daley, Cat Coore and Ibo Cooper of Third World. An (uncredited) Curtis Mayfield song that The Wailers had recorded before (details: 'Soul Revolution'), which now took on a new significance during Bob's gunman-enforced exile in London. Bob wistfully names his kids, and gives personal details of his family's finances (!) in a performance a long way removed from the defiance of the original cut.

EASY SKANKING Details: 'Kaya'

IS THIS LOVE

Horns mix. Details: 'Kaya', with added punch from a previously reduced-in-the-mix horn section.

SMILE JAMAICA

Co-authored by Lee Perry, who also concocted a dubbier mix than this one on two separate Jamaican Tuff Gong/Smile Jamaica 7" singles. 'Smile Jamaica' is a surprisingly sultry, slow celebration of Bob's birthplace recorded at the behest of Prime Minister Michael Manley for the Smile Jamaica concert. Bob was shot a few days before the concert. If Manley was expecting a jolly knees-up for the tourists, he must have been disappointed: this is almost a rebuke to a Jamaica that can't get it together to celebrate the good things in life. It was later used as the anthem of the Hurricane Gilbert relief concert in London, 1988.

TIME WILL TELL Details: 'Kaya'

CD 3

AFRICA UNITE Details: 'Survival' **ONE DROP** Details: 'Survival'

ONE DUB

Ringing, chunky dub version of previous entry. Originally the reverse side of 'One Drop' on Tuff Gong 7".

ZIMBABWE Details: 'Survival' **SO MUCH TROUBLE** Details: 'Survival' **RIDE NATTY RIDE** 12" mix. Extended from the original, with a brighter, more reverberating mix. Details: 'Survival' **BABYLON SYSTEM** Details: 'Survival' **COMING IN FROM THE COLD** 12" mix. Another dubby mix. Details: 'Uprising' **REAL SITUATION** Details: 'Uprising' **BAD CARD** Details: 'Uprising' **COULD YOU BE LOVED** 12" mix. A longer cut the equal of anything in the US discos at the time, and curiously similar to the spartan disco sound that Chic found stardom with in the same field. Details: 'Uprising' **FOREVER LOVING JAH** Details: 'Uprising' **RASTAMAN LIVE UP** Details: 'Confrontation' **GIVE THANKS AND PRAISE** Details: 'Confrontation' **ONE**

LOVE/PEOPLE GET READY 12" mix. A remix of the 'Exodus' version of the Studio One hit circa 1984. Details: 'The Wailing Wailers'/'Exodus'

WHY SHOULD I

Originally cut in 1971 for 1971, and never released, this was re-produced as a (less successful) single follow-up to 'Iron Lion Zion' in 1992. Another song of pride.

REDEMPTION SONG

Recorded live at Bob's last concert, 23 September 1980, in Pittsburgh Pennsylvania. Bob's brain tumour was diagnosed the day before. As acoustic as the version on 'Uprising', it's an uplifting stadium anthem all the way, but, conversely, a tear-jerker in this context.

BOB MARLEY & THE WAILERS: 'SONGS OF FREEDOM 15 TRACK SAMPLER'

TUFF GONG TGCS 1, AUGUST '92

Promo-only CD teaser for the box set. Tracks: 'Simmer Down', 'Put It On', 'Nice Time', 'Soul Rebel', 'Trenchtown Rock', 'Slave Driver',

'Burnin' And Lootin', 'No Woman No Cry (Live At The Roxy)', 'War', 'Jammin' (12" Mix)', 'Time Will Tell', 'Africa Unite', 'Coming In From The Cold', 'Could You Be Loved (12" Mix)', 'Redemption Song (Live)'.

BOB MARLEY & THE WAILERS: 'ALL THE HITS'
ROHIT RRLP 7757, US ONLY, JANUARY 1991

Well, almost none of the hits actually, but that didn't stop the album causing a huge stir in the collector's market when it was released at roughly the same time as the 'Talking Blues' LP. The album looks irredeemably cheap and nasty, and some of the titles are incorrect. But, damn, here is a pile of Marley rarities, the majority of which hadn't appeared on vinyl for years. Even those that had, such as 'Nice Time' and 'Hypocrites', weren't available with instrumental versions, which accompany each of the ten tracks.

Exactly where these tapes sprang from remains a mystery. The sleeve says 'Licensed from Bunny Lee. Used under permission of Rita Marley'. Since Bunny Lee, a veteran reggae producer, has a reputation of being able to achieve anything he wants to achieve in time, it should come as no surprise that he managed to put his hands on these tracks, drawn, incidentally, from the original two-track masters, not from records. The majority of the songs are Tuff Gong productions, although some, such as 'Thank You Lord' and 'Mellow Mood' date from before Tuff Gong existed, and were recorded for The Wailers' first self-owned label, Wail'N Soul'M. There's also a couple of Lee Perry produced tracks. Rumour has it that no-one was particularly happy about this

release, from Bunny Wailer to Island Records to Tuff Gong, who have threatened to issue the record on their own label. However, at the time of writing 'All the Hits' has been available for in excess of three years, and if no-one has stopped it by now, then chances are it will continue to remain available. It is, of course, greatly prized by Marley collectors.

Producers and musicians: various. Refer to track listing and original LPs for details.

REDDER THAN RED
Dating from circa 1973, this is a raw, slow skank that draws on the local slang of 'red' meaning red-blooded, strong and tough. Originally released on Tuff Gong as a single.

NICE TIME

The Wailers' classic rocksteady song of love and dancing from 1967. First released on Wail'N Soul'M in Jamaica, and Doctor Bird in the UK, the single was re-pressed by Tuff Gong in the mid-Seventies and has been a constant seller ever since. However, this version has been put through a somewhat crude echo device (crude because the whole track goes through one rather than just particular instruments), making it slightly different for collectors. And besides which, the instrumental cut has never been available before. Personnel include Lyn Taitt, guitar, and Tommy McCook's horn section. There is also a DJ (rap) version by Scotty in the vaults from around 1971, although it has yet to see release.

HYPOCRITES

The other half of the 'Nice Time' single, cut at the same session and almost as popular. The rhythm has been borrowed in reggae many times since, and Bunny Wailer covered it as 'Hypocrite' on 'Sings The Wailers'. The instrumental version is particularly good, full of fine, chunky guitar.

MELLOW MOOD

From circa 1968, released on WIRL as a single

(Jamaica), JAD (US). Another Wailers classic and one of Bob's best-remembered songs in Jamaica, Bunny Wailer remade it for 'Sings The Wailers' (1980), and it was also covered by Johnny Nash.

THANK YOU LORD

This is yet another rocksteady gem (1968), singing the praises of a God in pre-Rastafarian terms. Bunny and Peter's contributions are excellent, although Bob's is by far and away the highest voice in the mix. Originally issued on Wail'N Soul'M'. There's a later version on Trojan 45 which also appears on the 'In The Beginning' and 'The Very Best Of The Early Years 1968-74'.

MR CHATTERBOX

A fine and funky version of Studio One song 'Mr Talkative' from 1970, produced by Bunny Lee. Features Bob and Bunny Livingston only. Issued on the Jamaican and UK Jackpot labels, although the original pressings featured a spoken introduction between Bob and Bunny Lee, mildly disrespecting reggae producer Niney The Observer, not featured here.

I'VE GOT TO CRY

Correct title 'My Cup'. Produced by Lee Perry

circa 1970. Also to be found on 'Soul Rebels', without the instrumental version.

HEY HAPPY PEOPLE

Correct title 'Soul Almighty'. Production details as previous entry. Also on 'Soul Rebels' LP without the instrumental version. This cut is slightly longer with a few throwaway snatches of improvisation from Bob.

POWER & MORE POWER

Correct title 'Satisfy My Soul Jah Jah'. Originally a Tuff Gong single circa 1972. No relation to 'Satisfy My Soul'/'Don't Rock The Boat', this is one of the most uncompromising songs issued on Tuff Gong, a weighty, rough skank with some reedy, dry horns from what is probably Tommy McCook and A.N. Other. An unknown classic. The instrumental version had been virtually impossible to obtain until the release of this album.

I'VE GOT THE ACTION

Correct title: 'Try Me'. Production details as on 'Hey Happy People'. Also on 'Soul Rebels' LP without the instrumental version.

BOB MARLEY & THE WAILERS: 'NICE TIME'

ESOLDUN/LAGOON REG 1-115, DOUBLE ALBUM, CIRCA MARCH 1991

'All The Hits' packaged as a double LP with an improved cover, including a sleevenote from Frank Jacques. Details: 'All The Hits'.

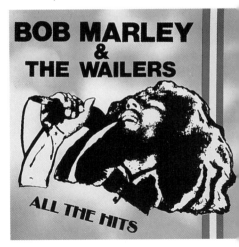

BOB MARLEY & THE WAILERS: 'THE UPSETTER RECORD SHOP - PART 1: THE COMPLETE SOUL REBELS'

ESSOLDUN/LAGOON LG2 1040, SUMMER 1992

A bizarre title for a Bob Marley album, with a faintly eccentric sleevenote and track listing to boot. However, the music, basically the 'Soul Rebels' LP remastered with the original two-track tape and with instrumental versions following each song, is unimpeachable, even if we've heard it all before. The running order is different from the original LP, and 'Memphis', an instrumental track anyway, isn't included. Tracks with different titles turn out to be nothing new, but collectors will not worry about it, being grateful instead for the few Marley tid-bits they are thrown, even if they are merely the backing tracks of songs they know and love.

Produced by Lee Perry. Details for all tracks: 'Soul Rebels' LP; tracks: 'Soul Rebels', 'Soul Rebels (Version)', 'No Water Can Quench My Thirst', (AKA 'No Water'), 'No Water (Version)', 'Rebel Hop' (AKA 'Rebels Hop'), 'Rebel Hop (Version)', 'No Sympathy', 'No Sympathy (Version)', 'It's All Right' (AKA 'It's Alright'), 'Reaction', 'Reaction (Version)', 'Corner Stone', 'Corner Stone (Version)', '400 Years', '400 Years (Version)', 'Make Up' (Correct title: 'My Cup'), 'Make Up (Version)', (AKA 'Version Of Cup'), 'Try Me', 'Try Me (Version)', 'Soul Almighty', 'Soul Almighty (Version)'.

BOB MARLEY & THE WAILERS: 'THE UPSETTER RECORD SHOP - PART II: RARITIES'

ESOLDUN/LAGOON LG2-1044, SUMMER 1992

The second LP of the pair is a real collectors' delight. Here's a heap of hard-to-find and never-before released masters, dating from between 1972 and 1977 (approx). There's some dispute as to the true provenance of the tracks: 'Concrete Jungle' and 'Screw Face' and 'Satisfy My Soul' are not Lee Perry productions at all, but Tuff Gong productions. The recording details are also a little erroneous: Randy's is certainly a studio where some of these tracks were cut, but 'WIRL' should read Dynamic, and 'Rainbow Country' was cut at neither, but at Lee Perry's Black Ark. As for the assertion that the records were produced at the back of Perry's record shop, from where the title of the two albums is derived, it's totally false, although doubtless Perry hatched what few marketing plans he had for The Wailers' tracks he had recorded somewhere within the confines of his retail premises. No matter, however, since words on record sleeves are never as important as the music on which they're supposed to inform. In this case, the music can speak perfectly eloquently for itself.

CONCRETE JUNGLE

The original version of the song that later turned up on 'Catch A Fire', and far more churning and harsh it is too, attempting to represent the hardships of life in what Kingstonians called the 'Dungle' in music. Dating from 1972, it was originally a US Tuff Gong 45, although this is a slightly different take to it.

CONCRETE JUNGLE (VERSION)

A stark instrumental cut of the above. Not to be confused with 'Ammunition', the other dub cut of the track on JA and US Tuff Gong 45s.

SCREW FACES

Correct title: 'Screwface'. Nothing to do with oral sex, but a comment on those eternal miseries who screw their faces up and make life hell for everyone else. The story here is not to be bothered by what anyone else says or does – a message that Bob, casting himself as a social outsider through necessity (as a Rasta and, originally within the span of his early career, a ghetto dweller), presented throughout his life. A Tuff Gong single (1972) and Punch (UK). This LP's version is, however, a different cut from the original pressings. Presumably produced by Bob Marley/The Wailers.

SCREW FACES (VERSION)
Instrumental cut of the above.

LOVE LIFE
Correct title: 'Love Light Shining'. One of the hardest-to-find Tuff Gong singles is given to all here. Produced by Lee Perry, circa 1971, it's a very laid-back, snail-slow skank. This cut is not, however, the same as that on the single, offering a more animated vocal from Bob, and far fuller backing singing from Rita as part of a chorus that does not sound like The Wailers. There's also a false start. The single took an altogether gentler approach.

LOVE LIFE (VERSION)
Instrumental version of the above.

SATISFY MY SOUL
Not 'Satisfy My Soul' as in 'Don't Rock My Boat', and not 'Satisfy My Soul Jah Jah' (Tuff Gong 7", 1972), although the rhythm track is the same as the latter, in a different mix. The vocal is a love song rather than a spiritual, and was seemingly pressed only on white label in Jamaica. A Tuff Gong production.

SATISFY MY SOUL (VERSION)
Instrumental cut of the above.

RAINBOW COUNTRY
A song that stands out from the rest in that it was cut in what was basically another era of reggae: 1975-76. 'Rainbow Country' was one of a bunch of masters that Marley cut at Lee Perry's Black Ark Studio at the time, of which about half have since emerged. The lyric for 'Rainbow Country' formed part of 'Roots Rock Reggae' (from 'Kaya'), and it's Bob at his most mystical, horns talking about wanting a dance, but in fact sounding like his mind is on far more esoteric matters:

Rasta as a natural part of the landscape. The broken, jagged rhythm, punctuated by lazy, almost stoned-sounding horn stabs, is Perry and Marley weaving a magic together, not dominated by either.

The track was released, slightly speeded-up, on Daddy Kool Records in Britain as a 12-inch, and on San Juan Records in America as a very scarce 7". It also appears on several cheapo European/British compilations with a bunch of other tracks that are endlessly recycled, such as tracks from the 'Soul Revolution'/Johnny Nash era. There is, incidentally, another mix of the track that's far closer to the sort of dub that Perry was putting together at the time, although it has yet to see release on anything other than an acetate.

RAINBOW COUNTRY (VERSION)

Instrumental cut of the above.

LONG LONG WINTER

Cut circa 1971 and produced by Lee Perry, 'Long Long Winter' is among the most obscure of Wailers tracks, based on a Curtis Mayfield song, no matter what the sleevenote may say.

Musically this is absolutely bare-minimum stuff, similar to the material on 'Soul Revolution', given body by the three-part Wailers harmonies.

LONG LONG WINTER (VERSION) Instrumental cut of the above. **PUT IT ON** Details: 'Soul Revolution' album. **PUT IT ON (VERSION)** Instrumental cut of the above. **DON'T ROCK MY BOAT** This mix is slightly different. Echo has been thrown onto the whole track, perhaps during mastering for this release. Details: 'Soul Revolution' album. **DON'T ROCK MY BOAT (VERSION)** Instrumental cut of the above. **KEEP ON MOVIN'** Details: 'Soul Revolution' album. This is an out-take with different vocals. **KEEP ON MOVING (VERSION)** Instrumental cut of the above.

BOB MARLEY & THE WAILERS: 'IN THE BEGINNING'
TROJAN TRLS 221, AUTUMN 1983

A grab-bag of oldies and obscurities featuring a bunch of songs that are only too familiar to Marley collectors together with a few real obscurities found lying around in the vaults. Sleevenotes are by Patrick Meads, Trojan's label-manager at the time, compilation is by Meads with help from David Hendley. Note: the details in the sleevenotes are frequently incorrect. Correct details follow. The album also forms part of the Trojan box set 'The Early Years 1969-73'.

SOUL SHAKEDOWN PARTY The most famous track from the Leslie Kong sessions. Details: 'The Best Of The Wailers'.

ADAM AND EVE
From around 1970, this biblical harmony song, giving women the burden of being "The root of all evil" is apparently drawn from sessions The Wailers cut for Dynamic, no matter what the sleeve might say. Also released on Jamaican 45 on Dynamic' Sounds' Tiger label, crediting The Bob Marley Singers.

BRAND NEW SECOND-HAND
AKA 'Secondhand', this obscure, gently menacing Tosh-fronted performance gives vent to a few grievances he's been storing up for an ex-girl-friend. Issued with a dub version as a single on the Justice League (Jamaica) and Upsetter (US) labels. Produced by Lee Perry, circa 1971.

CHEER UP Details: 'The Best Of The Wailers' album.

THIS TRAIN
The Wailers have another crack at the gospel song they first experimented with at Studio One (see 'One Love') LP. This lighthearted version was recorded for Dynamic, as the presence of The Dynamites band and the distinctive Dynamic studio sound makes evident, and released by The Bob Marley Singers on 7" single (Dynamic, Jamaica, 1970).

JAH IS MIGHTY

An alternate version of 'Corner Stone' (from 'Soul Rebels' LP). Slower, steadier, and a bit more eccentric, this was cut around 1970 for Lee Perry. Although it was pressed on a single, it didn't seem to get any further than white label.

CAUTION Details: 'The Best Of The Wailers' LP.

THANK YOU LORD

Betraying the distinct sound of Dynamic Sounds studio circa 1969-70, this somewhat bland cut of a song that Bob had several cracks at is gospel without fire. First issued on Dynamic 45 (Jamaica, 1970, crediting the Bob Marley Singers). Also released on Trojan 45 in a black bag at the time of Marley's death. The superior original is on 'Songs Of Freedom'/'All The Hits'/'Nice Time' and was a Tuff Gong 45.

KEEP ON SKANKING

Another obscure track, this record was something of a Holy Grail for Marley collectors on single until this record came out. However, since it was apparently never issued on single, it was a bit of a waste of time searching for it! Featuring Marley and Lee Perry on vocals, it was cut over Perry's 'Black Candle' rhythm (the original singer on the backing track was Leo Graham) for a dub-plate for British reggae producer Chris Lane. Lane was in Perry's Black Ark studio cutting dubs, when Marley happened by, and the track was cut on the spot, with Lane contributing some lyrics. A fine, but decidedly off-kilter Marley track, originally scheduled to come out on the Tuff-Set (ie Marley & Perry putting together their Tuff Gong and Upsetter companies) label as a single. Label and record, of course, never materialised. This is not, however, the only cut of the track recorded at the time: there's a much sparer mix, leaving Marley in a drum and bass desert. Lane also played bongo drums on the rhythm which Perry was going to release as 'Black Bongo'. It never came out. 1974.

WISDOM

Issued as the other side to 'Thank You Lord' in the UK (Trojan), 'Wisdom' is Bob in a very mellow mood. Production: Dynamic Sound, also issued on the Jamaican Tiger label in 1970 as the other side to 'Adam And Eve' as The Bob Marley Singers.

STOP THE TRAIN Details: 'The Best Of The Wailers'. **MR CHATTERBOX** Details: 'All The Hits'.

TURN ME LOOSE

An alternate, even-more stoned cut of the original version of 'Kaya' (details of original: 'Soul Revolution' album). Produced by Lee Perry, 1974, from the same session as 'Keep On Skanking'. Chris Lane should also get a writer's credit here, but doesn't. As with 'Keep On Skanking', there's also another, emptier version, as yet unissued.

BOB MARLEY & THE WAILERS: 'THE VERY BEST OF THE EARLY YEARS 1968-'74'

MUSIC CLUB MCCD 033, SPRING 1992

Another grab-bag of oldies, on CD only and at mid-price. Compilation and sleevenotes by the author. Tracks drawn from the Trojan archive. The only release where 'Small Axe' and 'More Axe', and 'Kaya' and 'Turn Me Loose' may be compared.

Tracks: 'Trenchtown Rock', 'Lively Up Yourself', 'Soul Almighty', 'Wisdom', 'Caution', 'Cheer Up', 'Thank You Lord', 'Stop the Train', 'This Train', 'Small Axe', 'More Axe', 'Don't Rock My Boat', 'Keep On Moving', 'Brand New Second Hand', 'Kaya', 'Turn Me Loose', 'Sun Is Shining', 'Keep On Skanking'.

BOB MARLEY & THE WAILERS: 'THE EARLY YEARS 1969-1973'

TROJAN CDTAL 60 4 CD SET, SEPTEMBER '93

A repackaging job from Trojan. 'Rasta Revolution', 'African Herbsman', 'In The Beginning' and 'Soul Revolution Volume 2' in a box, together with a 60-page large-format booklet with mid-Seventies pictures by Dennis Morris.

BOB MARLEY & THE WAILERS: 'CRYING FOR FREEDOM'

TIME WIND, HOLLAND 3 LP SET, DATE UNKNOWN, POSSIBLY 1984

A three-album box set of indifferent quality, repackaging much of the material to be found on other albums. There are other cheapo Marley box sets available. Generally speaking, they are better avoided, repeatedly recycling material from the Lee Perry, Leslie Kong and Sims/Nash/ Jenkins sessions, often with inferior mastering quality.

Tracks: LP 1: 'Mr Brown', 'Rebel's Hop', '400 Years', 'Soul Almighty', 'Lively Up Yourself', 'Small Axe', 'Trenchtown Rock', 'All In One', 'Keep On Moving'; LP 2: the entire 'Best Of The Wailers' LP; LP 3: the entire 'Soul Revolution' LP, including 'Keep On Moving', which already appears on the first LP of this set!

There are other CD box sets on the market in Europe at cut prices which rehash much the same material, plus, occasionally, 'Natural Mystic' (Lee Perry version) and 'Rainbow Country'.

BOB MARLEY: 'INTERVIEWS'
TUFF GONG, JAMAICA, RM007, AUTUMN 1982

Bob Marley interviewed by Jamaican journalist Neville Willoughby. With extracts from the following tracks: 'Natural Mystic', 'Trenchtown Rock', 'Redemption Song', 'Babylon System', 'Time Will Tell', 'Natural Mystic' (appears twice), 'Revolution', 'Survival', 'One Drop', 'Roots, Rock, Reggae', 'Guava Jelly', 'Rat Race'.

BOB MARLEY: 'I SHOT THE SHERIFF'
ON STAGE CD 12037, SPRING 1993

An Italian live album, taking advantage of the different copyright laws that prevail there. Supplies are sporadic, but it can be obtained through legal distribution throughout Europe at a fairly cheap price. Recorded live at the Quiet Knight Club, Chicago, 10 June 1975 in front of a very raucous, but what sounds like none-too-large crowd of aficionados. Marley's performance is fairly laid-back. Sound quality is like that of a reasonable bootleg.

Tracks: 'Trenchtown Rock', 'Rebel Music', 'Natty Dread', 'Midnight Ravers', 'Slave Driver', 'Concrete Jungle', 'Talkin' Blues', 'I Shot The Sheriff'.

BOB MARLEY: 'EXODUS'
ON STAGE CD 12002, 1991

The inferior of the two Italian live CDs on the On Stage label is not, of course, the same 'Exodus' LP that Island put out. Recorded at Ahoi, Rotterdam, 18 April 1980. Sound quality is passable.

Tracks: 'Is This Love?', 'Jamming', 'Easy Shanking' (sic), 'Get Up Stand Up', 'Exodus', 'No Woman No Cry', 'Positive Vibration', 'Crisis', 'I Shot The Sheriff'.

OB MARLEY & THE WAILER

RARITIES

E UPSETTER RECORD SHOP - PART II

RASTAMAN VIBRATION

BOB MARLEY
THE WAILERS

ALKIN'
LUES

Bob Marley and the Wailer

One Love

Bob
Marley

Peter
Tosh

Bunny
Wailer

at
Studio
One